Sign Language Made Simple

Karen B. Lewis and Roxanne Henderson

Illustrations by Michael Brown and Cassio Lynm

Produced by
The Philip Lief Group, Inc.

A Made Simple Book
Broadway Books
New York

A previous edition of this book was originally published in 1997 by Doubleday,
a division of Random House, Inc. It is here reprinted by arrangement with Doubleday.

Sign Language Made Simple. Copyright © 1997 by Doubleday,
a division of Random House, Inc.

For information, address: Broadway Books, a division of Random House, Inc.,
1540 Broadway, New York, NY 10036.

Broadway Books titles may be purchased for business or promotional use or for special sales.
For information, please write to: Special Markets Department, Random House, Inc.,
1540 Broadway, New York, NY 10036.

MADE SIMPLE BOOKS and BROADWAY BOOKS are trademarks of Broadway Books,
a division of Random House, Inc.

Visit our website at www.broadwaybooks.com

First Broadway Books trade paperback edition published 2001.

The Library of Congress Cataloging-in-Publication Data has cataloged the Doubleday edition as:
Lewis, Karen B.
    Sign language made simple/Karen B. Lewis and Roxanne Henderson:
  illustrated by Michael Brown and Cassio Lynm; edited and prepared for
  publication by The Philip Lief Group, Inc.— 1st ed.
        p.   cm.
    "A Made Simple Book"
    1. American Sign Language—Study and teaching. I. Henderson, Roxanne.
  II. Philip Lief Group.   III. Title.
HV2474.L48 1997
419—dc21   97-9233
                                                     CIP

ISBN 0-385-48857-2

18 17 16 15 14 13

Mary Feeney [signature]

Table of Contents

Sign Language

Made Simple

I. Introduction

What Is Sign Language?

Any person who studies a second language quickly learns that there is a great deal more to the task than "learning new words for things." Languages have their own structure, logic, and flavor — their own personality. They follow particular rules of use on everything from how to express tense (past, present, and future) to syntax (the order of the words), and many other elements. This is as true for sign language as it is for spoken language.

Or is it? Can handshapes and movements really be a form of language? Sure, people of all cultures use their hands to enhance their speech, and in some cultures hand gestures are used in well-defined and highly specific ways. Many international travelers have learned through embarrassing experiences that a gesture that means "A-OK" in one country is a rude vulgarity in another. Even so, these gestures are not language.

Sign is language, though, precisely because it is so much more than a collection of gestures. It is an organized set of rules and symbols used to communicate information, ideas, and feelings (which is actually a pretty workable definition of language in general).

This book focuses on American Sign Language (ASL), the major sign language used by deaf people throughout North America. As you move through this book and learn how to use ASL, the fact that it is a "real" language quickly becomes obvious. However, linguists and educators of the deaf have not always agreed on this point.

The English word *language* comes from the Latin *lingua* — which means, literally, tongue, and for a long time linguists considered the two to be inseparable. For much of this century, teaching programs for deaf children de-emphasized or even forbade signing. Educators of the deaf, meaning well, struggled valiantly to "normalize" nonhearing students by teaching them to use spoken English, at any cost. The cost, too often, was and is alienation and low academic achievement by deaf students.

Signing was thought to be a weak translation and therefore a poor substitute for the language of the signer's native culture. Real language was spoken and written, not "gestured." Signing was considered inferior, what people did if they couldn't master the real thing.

Signing was dismissed as mere picture drawing (iconography), efficient in what it did, but still not language. One could, however, make the same claim against spoken language. Consider the definition of *onomatopoeia*, i.e., a word that sounds like the thing it describes. *Buzz* is one, as are *hiss* and *zip*. Some theories about speech suggest that the first attempts by humans at spoken language were all onomatopoetic. Does that in any way debase our present-day speech? Of course not. Spoken language is much more than a string of onomatopoeia and sign language, much more than pictures drawn in the air. In fact, many studies have looked at whether signing is just pantomime, and they all arrived at the same answer: *No*. While some signs have a clear representational connection to the things they describe, others have a more tentative one, and just as often the connection is weak or nonexistent. Signing dictionaries, including ours, allude to these iconic connections, which may be useful as memory aids. But beyond that, making too much of the picture-link does tend to narrow the meaning of a sign that may have several related but nonidentical meanings.

While fluent signers use simple pantomime in humorous and poetic ways, and to spice up discourse in a metaphorical way, so do people everywhere in all forms of speech. But sign is not simply pantomime. If it were, anyone of minimal intelligence who paid attention could and would understand signs. In reality, nonsigners who observe signed discourse understand nothing or very little of it, and signers in one sign language do not automatically understand signs in another.

The truth is, our knowledge of the origins of many individual signs, just like our knowledge of many English words, is murky at best. What we know is that sign language first originated in residential schools for the deaf. Ironically, bringing deaf children together in groups, at least partially for the purpose of being taught spoken language, caused signing to flourish as never before. For most of the 19th century, sign language passed primarily from child to child, and in instances of a deaf child having a deaf parent, signing was passed down from generation to generation. Sign languages evolved as all languages do, idiomatically and idiosyncratically. To this day, little linguistic integrity exists beyond national borders, which usually also represent the boundaries of spoken languages. For instance, signers in France communicate differently from and cannot be understood by those in Germany. On the other hand, signers in the United States and Canada share pretty much the same ASL, although there are many regional differences.

These regional differences become obvious to the signer who learns ASL in one part of the country and uses it another. The author of this book, Karen B. Lewis, is an interpreter (not deaf, of course) and teacher of Sign and interpreting. She studied at Gallaudet University, in Washington, D.C., and has worked most of her signing career in North Carolina, where she interacts with the deaf and signers from all over the United States and Canada. Drawing on her vast experience, this book tries to span all regions of our nation; yet inevitably some signers will find some of our signs "foreign." We have not attempted to be utterly exhaustive or to list every ASL sign past and present, much less every small variation of these signs. That is a task we will leave to the academics and linguists. The goal of this compendium is to get the beginning signer started.

Which signs and variants to include has always plagued compilers of anthologies such as ours. One nonregional, universal sign language simply does not exist. Even within ASL, which is a fairly standard language throughout the United States and Canada, significant regional differences exist. The codifying and teaching of ASL — as well as its status as a legitimate language

— are just too new. Similarly, ASL has no standard, workable written form. Many academicians at various times have attempted to encrypt ASL, but the usefulness of this is considered to be very limited; after all, as written discourse, English will always be preferred. Overall, with the possible exception of what comes out of Gallaudet University (more on GU later), there simply is no "Queen's English" version of ASL, either on paper or in signing. It is first and foremost a language of face-to-face discourse.

Nevertheless, ASL does have an extensive vocabulary. It is highly organized and has a distinct set of rules concerning syntax (different from spoken English), usage, and so on, and is used to communicate everything in the world of facts, ideas, and feelings.

In the United States and all over the world people who cannot hear excel in reading and writing; they take advantage of and contribute to the huge body of culture and information available in print in many written languages. However, within the deaf culture, for off-the-cuff, on-your-feet "talking" and for the person-to-person discourse that is the stuff of our daily lives, the means of communication that best serves the deaf is Sign.

The Language of the Deaf Culture

Any notion that ASL is mere pantomime is now considered old-fashioned, even ethnocentric. Today, signing in general has become very accepted and respected. So much so that in fact, it was commemorated on a U.S. postage stamp printed in the 1980s. The hand on that stamp is signing "I Love You," which is a combination of the manual letters "I," "L," and "Y" and has come to be thought of as one of the basic ASL handshapes.

After much struggle by deaf people in the United States, ASL is now universally accepted as a distinct and legitimate language, independent of English (as is true of

ASL hits the mainstream — in the last decade, signs began to crop up in the most unexpected places: "I Love You" on a U.S. postage stamp.

other sign languages associated in other countries). This was a major milestone for the deaf for a very important reason: language and self-identity are inseparable. Just consider the debate in the United States over whether we should mandate an official national language, or the role that language (French versus English) played in the near secession of Quebec from Canada. Think of the fascist dictator Franco outlawing the Basque and Catalan languages after the Spanish Civil War. The language that an individual uses lies at the heart of his or her cultural identity. More than history, geography, or any other cultural quality, we are what we speak. The acceptance of ASL as a legitimate language has been critical to the people who depend on it daily.

After all, if you are what you speak, what does it mean to have your language dismissed as an irrelevant oddity? Deaf people, particularly those who lost their hearing before they developed spoken language skills, define an important part of themselves in terms of their unique culture and language.

Gallaudet University in Washington D.C. is the sole liberal arts institution dedicated to teaching the deaf in the United States. Gallaudet brought the deaf culture concept to national attention in 1988. That year, the deaf student population and faculty protested when the Board of Directors once again proposed to appoint a hearing president. Under massive protest, the Board backed down and appointed the University's first deaf President, I. King Jordan. It was during this public controversy that most people discovered that the deaf do consider themselves just like regular folks who can do anything anyone else can do, except hear.

And so, always keep in mind as you use this book that ASL *is not* just like English, only done with the hands.

Using This Book

Having established the uniqueness of ASL and how different it is from English, we admit we've had no choice in this book except to use English, along with detailed drawings, to help explicate the individual signs.

The majority of *Sign Language Made*

1

Simple is comprised of a "dictionary" of simple line drawings that show a person (head to waist) making a sign, along with an analogous English word, as well as special tips to help accurately form the sign. But do not proceed directly to the dictionary. It is important that you familiarize yourself (even memorize if you feel ambitious) the fingerspelled alphabet, a few additional handshapes, and the cardinal numbers from 1 through 9. These handshapes are laid out clearly in the charts contained in Chapter II. They are vital elements in learning ASL because they represent every handshape used in ASL discourse. However, the object of familiarizing yourself with the manual alphabet is *not* so that you start fingerspelling. If an ASL sign exists for a concept you wish to convey, you should be signing it, not fingerspelling it! The fingerspelling chapter will expand on situations in which you should or should not fingerspell, and there are tips throughout this book on how the use of fingerspelling fits into overall sign language.

Once you are familiar with all the basic handshapes, you will find it much easier to make the best use of the dictionary that comprises the bulk of this book. In the dictionary, we constantly refer to the handshapes by name (number or letter) in the written tips that accompany the line drawings. Following these handshape tips is a key ingredient in getting your sign right.

The dictionary itself is grouped not alphabetically, but by part of speech and by subject. First is a section on concrete nouns, followed by one on abstractions, and so on. Within these sections entries are organized by subject, to make topic-browsing easy. There are groupings devoted to food, colors, sports, and many other topics. At the beginning of each section we offer a brief explanation of some key signing issues related to that section. For instance, before the section on concrete nouns, we explain plurals and noun/verb pairs.

As a further aid to finding the sign you need, every sign that is illustrated in the dictionary or anywhere else in the book is indexed alphabetically by an analogous English word. This same index includes general subject entries, such as pronouns and plurals, so you can quickly locate help on various general subjects.

In addition, *Sign Language Made Simple* also includes some special and fun topics of interest, such as humor and idioms. Altogether, this book offers newcomers to ASL the tools needed to begin signing intelligibly on a basic level.

But, be warned — you cannot learn ASL from books alone, any more than you could learn to speak French using only a French-English dictionary. We do indeed devote a good deal of this book to a dictionary of signs; however, a list of words is not the same as continuous discourse. If you choose the equivalent signs for what you want to say in English, then construct them into an English-fashioned sentence, your literal translation will be "pidgin" at best. Though a fluent signer might understand some of what you meant to say, your signing would appear clumsy indeed. Along with the dictionary, make use of Chapter V, "Putting It All Together," which helps the beginning signer combine and use everything presented in the earlier chapters.

One limitation of any signing dictionary is that hand *movements* are difficult to convey in words or pictures. In our illustrations, we use directional arrows, and we try also to explain movements as clearly as possible in the accompanying written tips. Between these two methods, there should be little doubt as to the proper movement for any given sign, yet we realize that some room for error will probably remain.

Keep in mind that it is through hand movement, and also such elements as facial expression and body stance, that signers express their eloquence and poetry. Their passion and sense of rhythm reveal their very personalities and add nuance to the meanings of their signs. It is through the signs combined with the whole range of non-manual elements of signing, or markers, that the entirety of meaning is expressed.

Obviously, if you are studying Sign, it's because you know someone with whom you wish to communicate in this way. Let your deaf family and/or friends be part of your course of study from the beginning. These individuals will be your best source of all types of signs, including slang and idioms, as well as specialized and work-related signs. Needless to say, their help will be very important in getting you to sign like a "native."

A final note: just like any spoken language, ASL changes with the times and adds words to describe new fads and technology. This volume includes some versions of relatively modern signs (fax, contact lens, skateboard), but our real goal is not to present the cutting edge, but rather to offer a basic vocabulary and understanding on which to build. This book contains more than 1,200 illustrations of signs and hand-shapes. However, if you will be communi-

cating primarily with a coworker in a specific field, such as medicine, go to that person for help with your professional jargon.

Most of all, don't be shy. Like the inhabitants of any culture, signers are pleased when outsiders try to learn their language and thus understand their culture. With their help and the time you spend reading and studying this book, you'll be ready, when you next meet a fluent signer, to begin taking part in a unique and exciting form of conversation.

The following chapter starts off with the proper way to shape your hands to create signs, and explains the three other basic elements of signing correctly, namely hand location, hand movement, and palm orientation.

Now, let's get started!

II. What Is a Sign?

The Four Elements of a Sign

A single, complete sign is a symbolic representation of a thing, action, or concept. Each sign is made up of four distinct elements:

1. Handshape
2. Location of the hand in space in relation to the signer's head and torso
3. Movement
4. Orientation of the palm (whether it is facing up or down, or to the signer's right or left)

In order for a sign to convey the proper meaning, each of the elements must be done properly. *Each* element is important. Getting two or three right is not enough. Change one, and the whole meaning changes.

We'll start with the first element: handshape. But first, a note about right- and left-handed signing.

Which Hand to Use, Right or Left?

In the next few pages are many pictures of a disembodied right hand. For simplicity's sake, all the signers pictured here and throughout this book are right-handed. Our signers are all signing with their dominant (right) hands. If they were all left-handed, then most pictures in this book would be flopped like a mirror image, with what appears on the right now instead appearing on the left. Most, though not all, left-handed signers do with their left hands what our signers are doing with their right hands. If you are left-handed and find you are just as comfortable signing right-handedly, there's no reason you shouldn't. However, in general, don't switch hands during discourse! (You will learn, if you become truly expert at signing, that there are exceptions to the rule, but for now it will keep you in good stead.)

As the following illustrations show, no matter whether you are signing right-hand or left-hand dominant, you should use your dominant hand to carry out the primary action of the sign.

This is obviously true for signs formed with one hand alone, for instance, the sign *downstairs*.

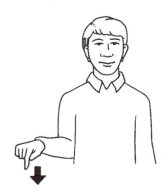

Downstairs

Here, the signer is indicating "downstairs" (or, depending on the context, just "down"). Obviously, he's signing right-handed.

It is true also for the many signs formed using both hands. When a sign is comprised of a primary and a supporting action, the dominant hand carries out the main action, as with the sign for *select*.

Select
This signer moves her dominant (right) hand from the index to the middle finger of the left hand; the left hand remains stationary, so you know she's signing right-handed.

Many signs are ambidextrous, that is, the right and left hands do exactly the same thing, in the same way, simultaneously. The following two signs express the concepts of *compete* and *language*.

Remember: If you are signing left-handed, perform the primary action with your left hand; if right-handed, use your right hand.

Compete

To sign "compete" both hands are in the "A" shape and both move quickly, alternating in and out; both palms face together.

Language

To sign "language" the actions of the hands mirror each other, too. Both these signs are done the same way, whether signed right- or left-handed.

Shaping the Hands

The many hands pictured on the next pages represent most of the finger/palm configurations (called *handshape*) used in ASL. Pictured first are the handshapes that correspond to A-Z of our written alphabet. This is called the *fingerspelled* or *manual* alphabet. There are several fingerspelled alphabets, but the particular one used by ASL signers, and shown here, is the American Manual Alphabet. Beginners should keep one important point in mind: A fingerspelled letter is not a sign, it is a hand-shape. And a fingerspelled word — the letters of the word spelled out by hand in English — also is not a sign, but a finger-spelled word. Fingerspelling is just another way to express English; Sign is a different language.

For instance, you fingerspell three letters to show the word *eye*. But to sign the concept of *eye* you form a single sign.

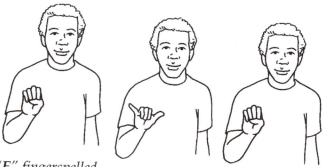

"**E**" *fingerspelled.*

"**Y**" *fingerspelled.*

"**E**" *fingerspelled.*

*The sign for "**eye**."*

While the fingerspelled alphabet can be used to spell out any word and is a legiti-mate method of communication, finger-spelling is time consuming, laborious, and less expressive than signing. More later, but for now, remember the difference.

After charting the fingerspelled alpha-bet, we show the additional handshapes used in forming ASL signs, which have descriptive names of their own, such as "claw" and "T/X".

Finally, we picture the handshapes for the numbers 1 through 9. These shapes are also routinely used in signing and are described by number. (The dictionary shows how to sign teens and higher num-bers, as well as ordinal numbers.)

Throughout this book, as we picture and explain how to form ASL signs, we will refer to particular handshapes by their names. We might instruct you to use an "X" or a flattened "O" handshape or an open "5" or a "1," or we might use its descriptive name (the "claw" hand, for instance). The illustration below, for example, shows the concept of *trade*. Beside it appears a signing tip that is fairly typical of the ones that appear in the dictionary entries of this book.

Any time you encounter a handshape in the text that is described by a letter or number, you can look up that shape in this chapter.

Trade

Both "F" hands; right hand starts close in, left out more from the body; then hands switch positions in and out.

You can see that knowing these handshapes is important. If you like, you may use these charts to practice each sign until you have them memorized before proceeding to the rest of the book. That's a good way to start feeling comfortable with using your hands in a new way, and it will give you a firm foundation in learning signs. Or, just familiarize yourself with each sign and try doing each one once or twice, then jump into the dictionary, learning as you go. Either way, you're probably going to want to stick a bookmark in this chapter and refer back to it often so you can make sure to keep your handshapes correctly formed.

But rest assured, sooner than you think, when you see an instruction to form, say, an "A" handshape, your four fingers will automatically bend down to your palm as shown in the first drawing in the first chart.

Remember: When using the dictionary in this book to form a sign, use both the illustration *and* the text to make sure your handshape is correct.

The Fingerspelled Alphabet

Here are the handshapes used by signers to spell the 26 letters of the alphabet. These drawings, like those showing the signers' half torsos, are shown from the point of view not of the signer, but of the person who is seeing the sign being formed.

A

B

C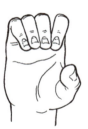

D

E

F

G

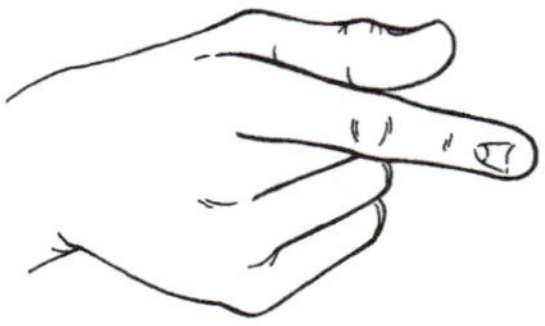

H

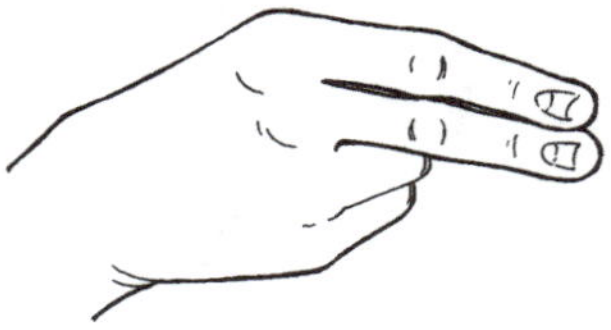

I

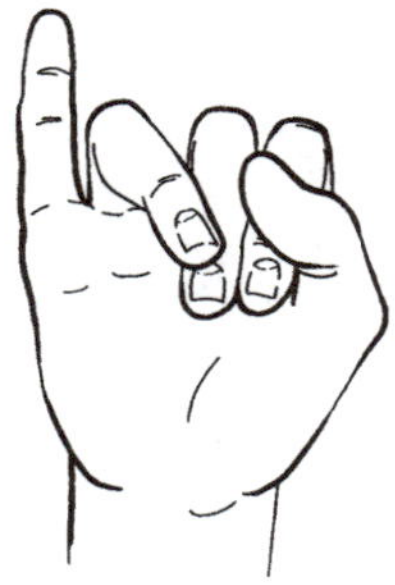

J

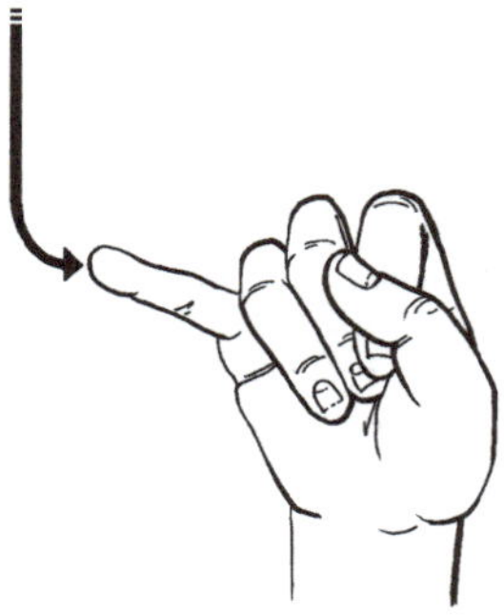

K

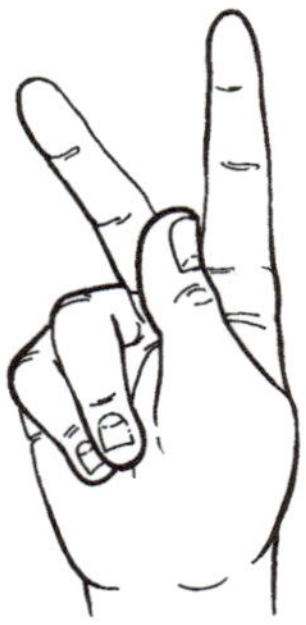

L

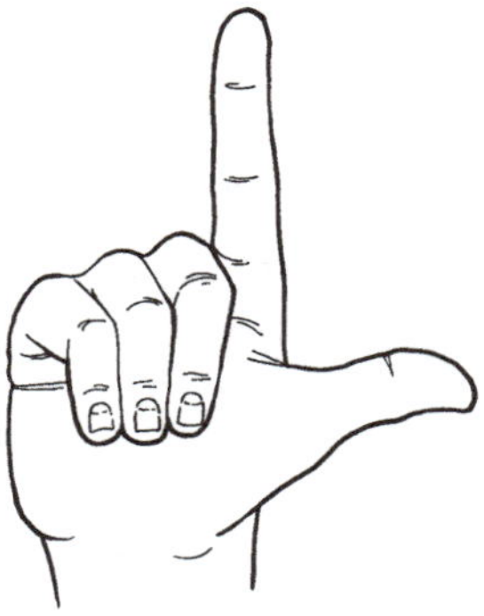

M

N

O

P

Q

R

S

T

U

V

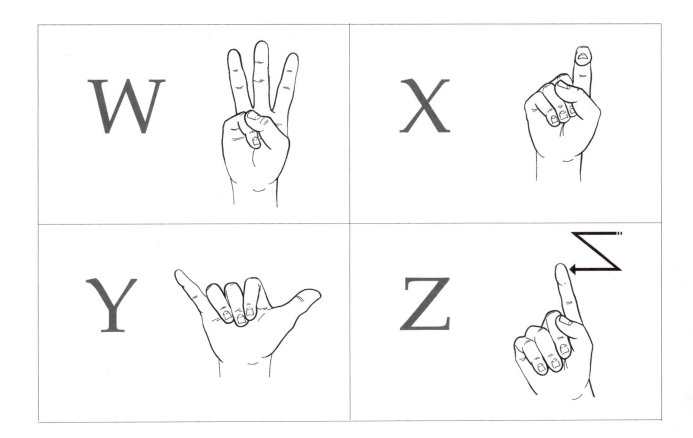

Other ASL Handshapes

Along with the fingerspelled letters, other handshapes are used in ASL, many based on the letter or number shapes. In addition to these shapes, the signing tips in the dictionary will sometimes describe other variations on the standard handshapes, such as bent "B" or closed "5." The chart below does not show all possible minor shape variations.

"C" with thumb and forefinger

Claw "5"

Slightly folded "5"

Flattened "F"

I Love You (I L Y)

Bent "L"

1-i	Bent "V" / Double "X"
Index	Sensing
Folded "3"	Flattened "O"
Closed "3"	Claw "3"

"Claw"

"T/X"

The Number Handshapes

Finally, here are pictures that show how to sign numbers in ASL. The numbers 1 through 9 actually function as handshapes and signs. They represent numerals, but they are also handshapes that are used in a variety of other signs, and we call them out in the text of the dictionary, just the way we call out letter handshapes, as guides in forming signs. Notice that some are variations on the fingerspelled alphabet. As in English, the teens, twenties, thirties, and so on are formed repetitively based on 1 through 9; examples are given later in the dictionary.

1

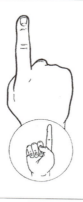

2

3

4

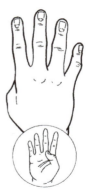

5

6

7

8

9

Hand Location

Got all those handshapes memorized? Well hang on, you still don't know how to sign.

Many books on signing have been published in the last decades, many presenting some sort of "dictionary" of illustrations, and some of them picture signs by showing only the hands. This is a mistake that can lead to confusion because even if you get the handshape right, it still matters very much where you place the hands in relation to your head and torso. In this book, every sign (except for those illustrating only *handshapes*) that is illustrated shows a *person* from the waist to the top of his or her head.

Exactly where you present the handshape — on your right or left side or directly in front of your torso; at head, shoulder, or chest height; or beside or in front of your mouth, ear, or collarbone — can change the meaning entirely. Pay attention or you could end up looking rather silly and saying very little. For example, the signs for *summer* and *ugly* and *dry* are identical in every way except in the location of the sign. All three have the same handshape, movement, and palm orientation. But note that *summer* is signed on the forehead, *ugly* on the midface, and *dry* on the chin.

Remember: When using the guides in this book to form signs, note the illustration *and* the text and make sure you are positioning your hand(s) in the correct location.

Summer

Ugly

Dry

In all three signs, the index finger of the right, "1" shaped hand moves straight from left to right and the hand closes into an "X" shape as it goes. What distinguishes these signs one from another is where they are signed in relation to the face.

Hand Movement

The third of the four elements of a sign is, as we talked about in the Introduction, one of the most difficult to show in two-dimensional drawings, that is, movement. Movement does not figure into some signs at all; these signs are stationary. However, when movement is present, it is a critical element. From sign to sign the hands may sweep, arc, circle, flutter, draw a line, describe a cube, wiggle, zig, or tremble. The directional arrows in the illustrations show what kind of movement should be made and whether it should go up to down or vice versa, right to left or left to right, clockwise or counter-, in a straight line or an arc, and so on. Pay attention to these arrows in the dictionary entries and to the tips that accompany each entry. Understand the required movement and don't fake it or improvise. Without the right movement the sign's meaning will change.

For instance, note that the signs for *Ireland* and *potato* have the same location, handshape, and palm orientation. Only the movement differs.

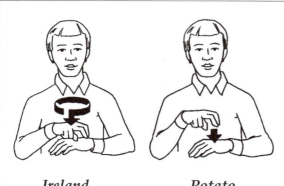

Ireland   **Potato**

The signs for "Ireland" and "potato" are both made in front of the body at midtorso, both use the bent, double "X" handshape, and both keep a palms-down orientation. However, for "Ireland" the right hand circles and comes down to the left; for "potato" the hand simply taps twice.

Another facet of movement that affects the meaning of a sign is the amount of vigor used. This can affect significantly the nuance of the meaning. For instance, look at the general sign for *storm*. If this young lady were talking about a real tree-tossing hurricane, she would alter her back-and-forth movement and maybe even indulge in some pretty wild hand swinging. It's okay to improvise in the expression or degree of vigor of the movement as long as you don't change the type of movement.

Storm is a fairly pictographic sign. Many signs like this allow a lot of latitude in the energy or vigor of the movement. The many dictionary entries in this book show you how to do these in a most general way. It is up to you to tailor the sign to the particular circumstances of what you are trying to say. After you've tried a sign like *storm* in the most general way, think about its visual

effect, and sign it once more, with greater or lesser intensity.

Remember: When using a dictionary entry to form a sign, note the arrows in the illustration *and* any extra advice in the text about movement. Be careful how you make the movement.

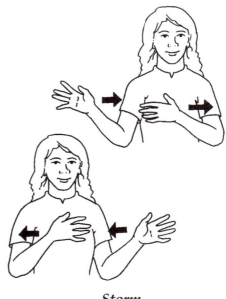

Storm

She's describing a fairly mild storm; the more vigorous the movement, the more violent the storm.

Palm Orientation

The fourth element of the sign is the orientation of the palm. Your handshape can be correct and your movement and location proper, but if you turn the palm in when it should be out, or left when it should face right, you are not signing what you intended to sign.

For instance, the following two signs both use the "S" handshape, are signed in the front of the body at midtorso location, and tap the right and left wrists together. The only difference is that in the first sign shown, the left hand is palm down and in the second one the left hand is palm up. The first sign is *job*, the second means *rough sex* or in some places *rape*. These are not two signs that you can use interchangeably.

Remember: When using the dictionary to form a sign, note the palm orientation in the illustration; it is often reiterated in the text, too. Correct palm orientation is essential.

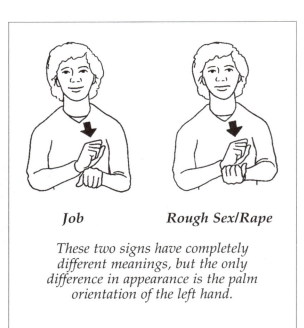

Job   *Rough Sex/Rape*

These two signs have completely different meanings, but the only difference in appearance is the palm orientation of the left hand.

The Relationship Between Fingerspelling and Signing

Not all English words have analogous signs. Few proper nouns, for instance, have their own signs. While a sign exists for *soap* or *detergent*, you would fingerspell a brand name such as *Ivory*. Similarly, there's a sign for *automobile*, but not for *Subaru*. A general rule is that objects, concepts, or actions that are extremely specific will often be expressed through fingerspelling. You would sign *dance* but, for more specificity, fingerspell *clog*. However, it is not unusual at all for a close group of signers who work or play together to develop their own signs for matters common to them that are not often expressed by other signers.

But how do fledgling signers know when to "resort" to fingerspelling? First of all, unless you learn fingerspelling and learn it well, this is not a bridge you are ever likely to cross. Fluent signers are able to fingerspell at a rate that far exceeds the comprehension rate of nonfluent individuals. Should you take it upon yourself to learn this practical skill, the chart of the manual alphabet given in this chapter will serve you well. However, you are going to need to practice with and get feedback from a fluent fingerspeller. This book concentrates on ASL and is not intended as a fingerspelling instruction manual.

Having said that, here are some general guidelines for those instances when fingerspelling is the thing to do: names of people and animals, cities, states, counties, and so on (there are signs for many countries); titles of movies, plays, and other works of literature and art; and brand names.

Here are a few other things to remember about fingerspelling:

- Fingerspelling is a component of sign language, not a language unto itself.

- The hand stays in one place, with the elbow down, near shoulder height.

- The palm of the hand generally faces the receiver.

- The hand and wrist move and the forearm moves slightly (but not the entire arm as it can when forming signs).

- Fingerspelling flows like a motion picture. It is not presented one frame at a time. One letter transitions smoothly into the next. A fingerspelled word is a unit, like a printed one is. Adept fingerspellers see whole words the way readers do, not the individual letters of the word.

- There are very slight pauses, as in speech, between fingerspelled words.

Finally, a note about an interesting sort of hybrid sign referred to as a *fingerspelled loan sign*. The fingerspelling of a number of short (two- to five-letter) and commonplace words evolved (or condensed, you might say) over time into signs that are now accepted as signs in their own right. Examples include *yes, no, dog, 21*, and there are many more. You may notice other examples throughout the dictionary as your proficiency grows, but many, like the sign for *yes*, have come from their roots.

Yes, pictured below as it is signed today, retains very little of the letters *Y, E*, and *S*. But indeed, it is a descendant of what was once the standard way (fingerspelling) to express *yes*. What remains is the movement (a forward nodding that does suggest the movement of fingerspelling), the location (it is signed at the location where you fingerspell), and the handshape ("S," the final letter in *yes*). While there's no direct analogy for the fingerspelled loan sign in English, it does bring to mind abbreviations and contractions.

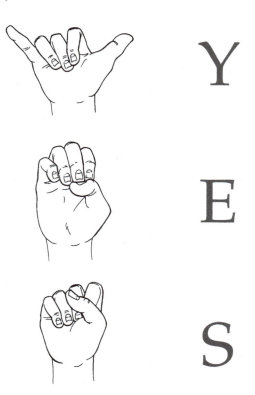

Y

E

S

Yes

A fingerspelled loan sign started out as a commonly fingerspelled word, then its manual letters eventually "blurred" or melded into a discrete ASL sign.

Remember: If you practice fingerspelling in front of the mirror, you'll be learning how to read signs at the same time. Have fun!

III. Elements of a Rich Language

Non-manual Elements of Sign

When learning to sign, you will concentrate first on getting the handshape, hand movement, hand location, and palm orientation correct. This is natural and necessary, but as you go along it also becomes important to pay attention to some other ingredients of proper signing. These elements are often referred to as the non-manual elements of signing, and they consist primarily of *facial expression* and *eye contact*. Don't underestimate the importance of the non-manual elements; they contribute significantly to the meaning of the sign.

Facial Expression

Lively, varying, and appropriate facial expression is an important part of *any* form of face-to-face communication. In Sign, however, facial expression serves literally as a grammatical aspect of the language. Signers rely heavily on facial expression to communicate nuances and shades of meaning. When a signer uses his or her face to underline the meaning (or suggest a specific connotation) of a sign, it helps the viewer immeasurably in quick comprehension of what is being signed.

For instance, signing a question word (when? who? what? and so on) *requires* that the signer wear an "inquiring" expression.

Signers always sign questions with a questioning expression on their faces.

In sign language, facial expression serves the same role that voice volume and tone serve in spoken communication. The meaning of spoken words can change entirely merely with a change in how those words are spoken. Say "Oh yes, I really love him" with sincerity, and it means exactly what the words say. Say it with sarcasm, however, and it takes on the completely opposite meaning. Similarly, in spoken language you can turn nearly any statement into a question, with no change in the words or the order of words, merely by raising your voice at the end of the sentence: "You have two dollars," versus "You have two dollars?"

This kind of mutability of meaning also exists in sign language. If a signer wishes to have his or her complete meaning understood (for example, to express not just regret, but sincerely felt regret, or not just awareness, but sympathetic and caring awareness, or not merely anger, but fury, not distaste, but revulsion), the signer must accompany or parallel the signs with the right facial expressions in order to nail down the meaning and nuance.

Naturally, the eyes and eyebrows play a big part in this. For instance, signers narrow their eyes or raise their brows to imply that a question is being asked. In a different context, raising the brows can also indicate sympathy. In either case, the intensity of the facial expression indicates the intensity of feeling, and the combination of sign and facial expression together convey the signer's full meaning.

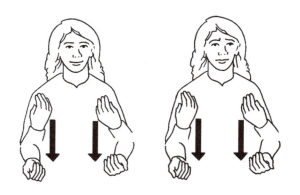

Now   *Now?*

The signer squints, and next raises her brows to indicate that she is asking a question, not making a statement.

"Sorry,"signed with a mild expression to indicate regret in a neutral sort of way.

"So sorry," signed with brows up and with such a sorrowful expression that clearly the signer means this is a sincere, heartfelt apology.

Whereas raising the brow shows curiosity or sympathy, wrinkling the brow and/or frowning expresses negation. You might do this when you are offering an opposing opinion, or whenever replying *No* to any kind of inquiry. Similarly, scrunching up your face is a way to communicate anger or intensity. In every case, the intensity of facial expression should mirror the level of feeling you wish to present.

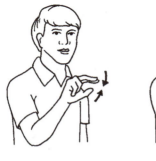 

No   *No!*

This fellow has just been asked to the movies. His first "No" is fairly neutral; he's just too busy that night. The way he expresses the second "No" is more like, "No, never, no way!"

The use of facial expression is not, of course, unique to sign language. Many different kinds of facial expressions are used as part of spoken communication in all cultures around the world. Signers naturally make use of the same range of expressions as their non-signing compatriots, and they use these to great effect in signing: blinking for surprise; the double-take of incredulity; the wink that says "I'm just joking"; crossing the eyes for comic effect; rolling the eyes in exasperation; sticking out the tongue in mock insolence; and on and on. Whether restrained or exaggerated, each signer (or speaker) will spice and flavor their discourse with facial expressiveness in his or her own way, depending on their temperament.

It is important to remember, however, that in signing, the use of proper facial expression is not merely an *option*, as it is in vocalization. It is much more acceptable and understandable for a *speaker* to talk deadpan and in a monotone; they can let the words speak for themselves. In signing, however, facial expressiveness is much more important. If you fail to communicate with your face as you communicate with your hands, what you are signing may be incomprehensible. Those to whom you are signing will not know whether you are asking a question or making a statement, whether you are being sincere or pulling their leg.

Remember: Use the appropriate facial expressions.

Eye Contact

Given the nature of this visual language, eye contact during signing must be slightly more formalized than in speech. It is polite for the receiver to maintain eye contact and give the signer full attention.

Think about the etiquette of spoken language: an attentive, interested listener will "hang on every word" of a speaker. Meanwhile, the speaker may move his or her head and shoulders, turn back and forth, gesture, or even look away. An uninterested and perhaps deliberately rude listener may turn away and stop looking at the speaker, showing that their attention is wandering, although he or she is still listening.

In signing, however, if you are being signed to and you look away, you have distinctly broken off and completely absented yourself from the discourse, the equivalent in spoken conversation of clapping your hands over your ears. Furthermore, if you look away from the person who is signing to you *and* simultaneously begin signing, you are blatantly interrupting. If, for instance, you look away while being signed to and give your attention to a passing entourage of Hare Krishna devotees, the signer will immediately stop signing and follow your gaze. Is this rude of you? A bit, but probably understandable, under the circumstances.

While it is polite of receivers to keep their eyes on the signer, it is quite acceptable for the signer to repeatedly break eye contact and reestablish it at will. This may be done for intensity or to underline the fact that they especially do not want to be interrupted at that particular moment. They do not, in a sense, want their "performance" interrupted.

In fervent signing or spoken discourse, a group of people who are communicating may all occasionally and briefly sign/talk at the same time. If you reach the point in your signing ability where you can hold your own in this type of situation, congratulations! Inevitably, all parties cannot actually manage to pay attention, listen, and receive all at once, and a situation in which no one accepts the receiver/listener role will quickly degenerate into confusion.

In reality, any type of conversation, whether signed or spoken, does not consist of people taking turns making speeches: John holds forth while Grunildahide waits and attends, then Grunildahide has her say with John passively listening. Real conversation (the reason, after all, that sign language came to life) is a give-and-take affair. When people really converse, it is a rat-a-tat business that in a sense has more in common with dancing than with speech making.

In addition to the all-important eye contact, eyes are also used as a means of adding emphasis. For instance, narrowing your eyes while making a sign is a way to say *very*. This holds true to some extent also with spoken language. Imagine saying to someone that you had just eaten the most delicious truffle of your life; you might well close your eyes while saying, *Sooooo delicious*. However, this element once again has a more preeminent role in Sign. Adding emphasis by narrowing the eyes in signing is not only effective as a qualifier, it's an efficient grammatical tool, a simple way to change the meaning of, for instance, *cold* to *frigid*, or to make the sign for *old* mean *elderly*.

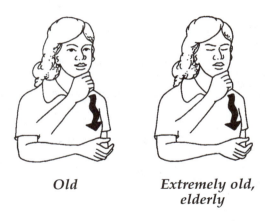

Old | *Extremely old, elderly*

The sign for "old," when formed with eyes closed for intensity, indicates a change of meaning to "elderly."

Remember: When watching a signer, maintain eye contact.

Compound Signs

Compound signs are common in ASL. Many illustrations of compound signs appear among the entries in the signing dictionary of this book, and a compound sign is immediately apparent when you flip through the dictionary: these entries are comprised of two or more drawings of the hands and sometimes require two or more complete drawings. This amount of detail is necessary to communicate the sign accurately because a compound sign actually consists of two or more signs combined to form a separate and different sign. The compound sign that is formed will always relate in some way to its constituent signs. Sometimes it will be a matter of simple addition; for instance, *water + melon = watermelon.*

The sign for "watermelon" is comprised of the sign for "water" followed by the sign for "melon" or "pumpkin."

Water

Melon

Other times, a compound sign is more than the sum of its parts, and more blending is required to arrive at the meaning. *Flood* (*water* plus *rise*) is a good example.

Water   **Rise**

"Water" combined with the sign for "rise" means "flood."

Signs can combine in even more oblique ways to form a compound. For instance, combining the signs for *chair* and *length* results in a sign that means *couch* or *sofa.*

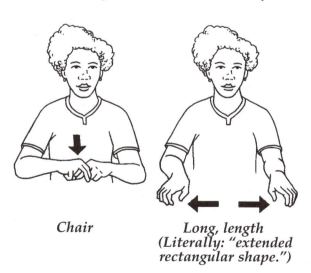

Chair   *Long, length (Literally: "extended rectangular shape.")*

Together these two signs add up to mean "couch" or "sofa."

Some signs are used so frequently in forming compound signs that they take on a grammatical identity of their own. These can be very useful tools in expression and in vocabulary building. The sign for *person* is a good example.

Person is so often combined with one or more other signs to form a compound that the sign has come to be called the *person marker*. The person marker, when added to another sign, functions in a way similar to how adding the letters ER functions in English. That is, the person marker sign, combined with a sign for a thing or action, creates a sign for a person who does or exemplifies that thing.

Person

The sign for "person" is used to indicate a generic individual.

For example, add the person marker to *baby* and *take care* to form *baby-sitter*; or, to *count* to form *accountant*; or *army* to form

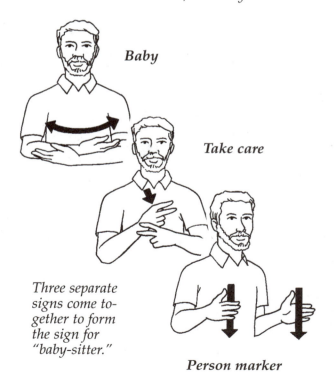

Baby

Take care

Three separate signs come together to form the sign for "baby-sitter."

Person marker

Count   **Person marker**

Army   **Person marker**

The person marker, added to the sign for "count" means "accountant"; added to the sign for "army" it forms "warrior/soldier."

warrior/soldier. There are many examples of compounds that are formed by adding the person marker to another sign. In fact, as you grow in confidence as a signer you can add the person marker to any other sign you wish, as long as the result can easily and quickly be understood without confusion. For instance, add it to *drive* and you have *driver*. But add it to *cat* and what do you have? A cat person? A cat woman? A cat keeper? Make sure that your meaning — the human occupation or endeavor being described — can immediately be grasped.

Another commonly compounded sign is the one for *room*. Alone, this sign means a room, any room, the concept for a generic room. However, *room* can also be combined with many other signs to describe many more specific rooms.

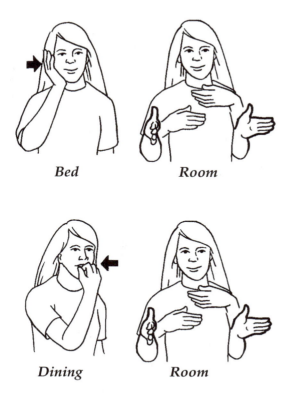

Bed   *Room*

Dining   *Room*

Using the room marker you can describe every room in the house, every room that you can imagine, in fact.

Note: When used to mean an *individual* and *not* compounded with another sign, the *person* sign may be formed with the "P" handshape, or the hands may be straight and flat in the closed "5" shape. When used as part of a compound, though, the person marker should *not* be formed with the "P" shape. The same is true for *room*; it is preferable to drop the "R" handshape when using this sign as a compound. (Read on in this chapter for more on "initializing" signs.)

Gender of Signs

Another interesting aspect of ASL is that many of the signs have a sort of "gender," as French and other Romance language words do. Notice that when a sign has to do with a man or a boy, it will nearly

always be located or touch upon the upper face, somewhere from the middle of the nose up to the top of the forehead. Signs associated with a woman or a girl, on the

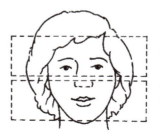

Male

Female

Gender Areas
The location of a sign can indicate the gender of the thing being signed, with "male" signs occurring on the upper face, and "female" on the lower.

other hand, will be located on the lower face, from just above the nostrils down to the bottom of the chin.

Gender in signs is useful in a couple of ways. For instance, signs describing similar but gender-different family relationships are signed with the same handshape, palm orientation, and hand movement, as with *brother* and *sister* for instance. All that changes is the beginning location of the sign.

Brother   *Sister*
For the male and female signs, only the location near the face is different.

For a gender-neutral concept such as *cousin*, the signer will actually modify the sign by placing it either at the lower or upper face, depending whether it's a male or female cousin. This is a peculiarity of expression not usual in English.

Remember: The gender of signs can help you to tell some of them apart (like *father* and *mother*) and thus to remember them more readily.

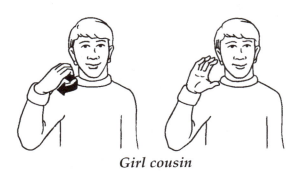

Girl cousin

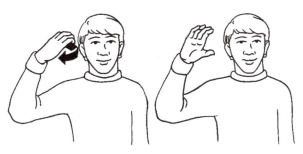

Boy cousin

Natural and Initialized Signs

In the Introduction we talked about iconography and whether signs were just pictures or pantomime. It remains important to make the point that there is a great deal more to Sign and to ASL than picture drawing. However, ASL does have a pictorial aspect, and some of the long-accepted signs are good examples of how iconography has been an important building block in the formation of ASL. An iconographic or "natural" sign is indeed a simple, elegant,

visual representation of a concept being signed. Three good examples, pictured below, are: *listen*, *pet*, and *eat*.

Here are the signs for "listen," "pet," and "eat" — not pictured in this order, but you can easily tell which is which.

Many other signs, however, rather than being clearly "natural," only vaguely draw a picture of the concept being signed, or not at all. In the previous chapter we described the relationship between fingerspelling and signing and when to use fingerspelling of English words in ASL discourse. The manual alphabet has another vital role in ASL. In addition to being a catalogue of handshapes and being used for fingerspelling proper names and so on, it is woven into ASL for use in forming initialized signs.

An initialized sign is one in which the handshape is the first (initial) letter of the analogous English word. This is very useful in ASL in distinguishing between signs that have related but different meanings. For instance, the signs for *music* and *poetry* have the same location, movement, and palm orientation, but the shape is different. *Poetry* is signed with a "P" and *music* with an "M" (illustrated on the following page).

"Poetry" with a "P"   *"Music" with an "M"*

Other examples of signs where initialization is used to make meaning changes are *respect–honor, family–department,* and *restaurant–cafeteria.* There are many others throughout this book, and more are continually incorporated into ASL as its vocabulary expands.

Honor

Change the hand-shape to "R" and the sign means "respect."

Department

With an "F" handshape this sign means "family," "T," "team," and "O," "organization."

Cafeteria

With an "R" hand-shape the sign is for "restaurant."

Remember: Initialization distinguishes related but different signs from each other and can help you remember signs.

Modified Signs

Like initialized signs, modified signs are formed when the signer makes a deliberate change in how the sign is formed in order to qualify its meaning. When a signer modifies a sign, however, he or she does not so much *change* the meaning as to make it more specific. The sign for the verb *close* is a good example.

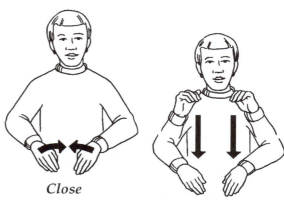

Close   **Close the window**

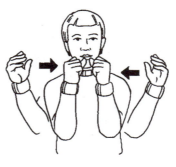 

Close the curtains

Close the book

Modifying the sign for "close" changes how the sign is formed to more accurately describe the context.

The sign presented in our dictionary means *close* in a somewhat generic sense, signifying perhaps to *close* the store. However, in the event that you are making this sign in the context of closing a specific physical thing, you will want to modify how you use that sign. If, for instance, you wish to describe closing a window, curtains, or a book, you would modify the sign to show more closely that exact act of closing.

Another good example of modifying a sign can be seen in the different ways you can sign *climb*. The generic *climb* pictured in the dictionary might reasonably and logically represent the climbing of a ladder. However, if the context were climbing a tree or rope, you would modify your formation of the sign accordingly.

The point is not to be rigid and wooden about signing. Yes, it is important to get each of the four elements of a sign correct, but sign is a visual language. Does it make sense to tell a story about Aladdin climbing a rope into thin air by using a sign that is clearly meant to show ladder climbing? Or, when relating an anecdote about the Senator making a speech with his fly down, would you sign *zipper* at midtorso? Where's the humor in that?

Remember: Let context guide you in modifying signs to be more descriptive.

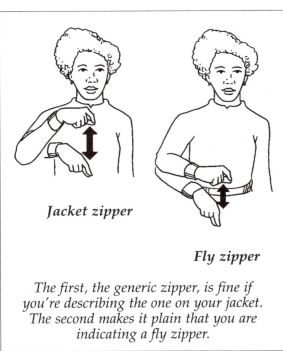

Jacket zipper

Fly zipper

The first, the generic zipper, is fine if you're describing the one on your jacket. The second makes it plain that you are indicating a fly zipper.

Climb a ladder

Climb a tree

Climb a rope

The sign for "climb" will look different depending on what is being climbed.

Personal Differences

People come in all shapes and sizes. Some are long in the torso, some long legged, while some have proportionately short arms or narrow or wide shoulders. Individuals also have varying levels of dexterity in their hands and fingers, and certainly no two people who ever lived have had identical temperaments or personalities.

Even if a person faithfully forms a sign according to its four prescribed elements, his or her personal physical and psychological attributes will affect the appearance of the sign to some degree. In the same way that speakers may hurry their words or be very expressive emotionally, so will signers vary in expressiveness. No two signers will express themselves exactly alike in the formation of the same sign. In fact, the more fluent a signer is (as is true with any language), the easier it becomes for him or her to use that language with personal style and still get it right.

It takes a while for any language student to reach that level of facility. In the meantime, try out your new ASL skills, and communicate in Sign with as many people as you can so that you'll become accustomed to differences in personal style.

Regional Variations

The next section of this book is the Dictionary of ASL Signs. Before you plunge your hands into this rich language, remember one more thing, something we mentioned briefly in the Introduction: regional differences. As you communicate with more signers you invariably will run up against some real differences in vocabulary.

While your inexperience may sometimes be the culprit, remember that significant regional differences continue to exist in ASL. These differences can occur over small geographic areas, so be prepared to learn as you go, and don't let it throw you. The more folks you sign with, the more you'll notice

that we don't all sign the same up North as we do down South, or in the West, or in Canada. For instance, notice how *Coke* is signed in many parts of the South.

This is something of an old-fashioned colloquialism, indicating that the drink is a "pick

Coca Cola, Southern style

me up" or "shot in the arm." Today, through much of the rest of North America, Coca Cola, following the trend common with other brand names, is fingerspelled. The sign illustrated here for *Coke* currently more widely means *to give* or *receive a shot* outside the South. If you are signing with an old-timer in Pittsboro, North Carolina, great. But most other places, it will be better to stick with fingerspelling for this one.

As another example, look at the following three signs for peaches.

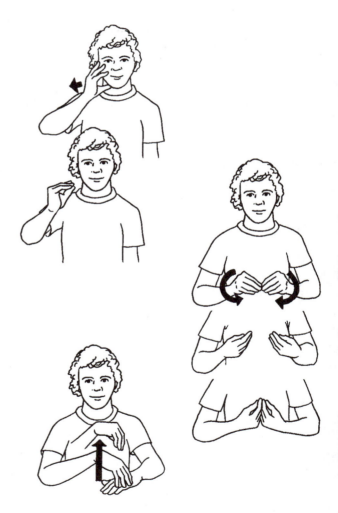

Three different signs for "peaches," used in different parts of the United States and Canada, all perfectly acceptable.

An Evolving Language

Along with regional differences, you may also encounter some generational differences. Sign, like any other language, evolves over time, with individual signs undergoing changes in one or more of the four elements. Although exactly how a single sign might change is unpredictable, signs tend to become more economical in movement as they change. There are, for instance, two separate signs for *student* that you might encounter.

It will be helpful to you to try to think of regional differences not as obstacles, but as one of the features of ASL that makes it a rich language. There was a time when spoken English in North America retained many more regional distinctions than it does today, and this fact is a source of sorrow to many. Maybe language was a little more interesting when you said *"tomaytoe"* and I said *"tomahtoe..."*

Give yourself a break. As you sign, don't be afraid to make mistakes. Don't hesitate to ask questions, expect confusions to occur, and most of all, have fun.

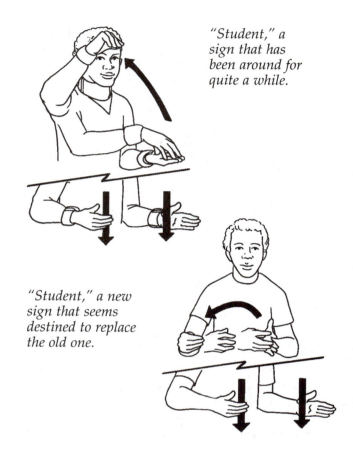

"Student," a sign that has been around for quite a while.

"Student," a new sign that seems destined to replace the old one.

IV. Dictionary
of ASL Signs

Concrete Nouns

Abstractions

Action Verbs

Describers

Other Parts of Signing

1. Concrete Nouns

The Signs for:
- *People*
- *Body, Health, Sickness, and Hygiene*
- *Work, Study, Art, and Money*
- *Play, Leisure, and Travel*
- *Food and Eating*
- *Places and Furnishings*
- *Time and Climate*
- *Animals and Plants*

Special Issues

Finding the Sign You Seek

Like words, certain signs serve several functions: as nouns, verbs, descriptors, and so on. This dictionary is arranged in order of those uses, called "parts of speech" in English. The advantage of organizing our library of signs in this way is that it will make it easier for many students to grasp and remember entire small groups of closely related signs. For instance, the days of the week appear together, not alphabetically, and they are similar in formation. The same is true for related signs such as *mother* and *father*, and *daughter* and *son*.

Verbs appear later in the dictionary, and they too, particularly action verbs, are grouped together within that section by subject, and you will immediately notice similarities among certain groups of verbs. For instance, verbs describing methods of communication (*announce*, *argue*, *lie*, and so on) all have similar handshapes and locations.

Noun/Verb Pairs

Another advantage to this subject-oriented organizational method is that the reader (or browser) always knows by an entry's location what function the sign serves. For instance, if it's in the verb section you know that the sign for *close* means to *shut*, not *nearby*. However, there is a special exception that you should keep in mind, namely, the case of noun/verb pairs.

A noun/verb pair is easy to define: it is a single sign that functions as both a noun and a verb. How then, will you know, when you see someone sign one of these noun/verb pairs, whether their intent is as a noun or a verb? Context, for one thing, but more importantly, the signer will alter the sign just a bit depending on its function. In every way but one, the sign will be formed the same, whether describing a thing or an action. The difference is: when a noun/verb sign is used as a noun, the movement (whether a tap, circle, flick, or whatever) is performed repeatedly, usually twice. However, if the sign is used as a verb, the signer only makes one continuous movement. Throughout the dictionary, in both the noun and verb sections, we draw attention to noun/verb pairs by a note in the signing tip.

If you are now wondering how we decided where to place each of these multi-purpose signs — in the noun or verb section — we must admit that the decision wasn't very scientific. Sometimes the placement in one section or the other seemed natural and logical, since the sign/word was one that has a primary use as a noun or a verb, but many choices were simply arbitrary.

In any event, whenever you are looking for a sign that is analogous to a particular word in English, remember that the alphabetical index at the end of the book can lead you to it.

Plurals

There are several ways to form noun plurals in Sign.

- *Repetition.* Make the sign twice or several times to indicate that there are two or more of the objects.

- *Qualifying.* Before signing the noun, sign *many*, *some*, *several* or any other qualifier that indicates more than one.

- *Pointing.* If the sign you wish to pluralize is a person or thing to which you are referring by pointing, then point multiple times to several spots. This will indicate *them*. Or, you may point to the one thing and then sweep your hand to indicate/encompass the whole lot of them.

International Signs

The signs that appear in this book are ASL. There is no universally used sign language (unless you count Gestuno, a kind of sign Esperanto created for international use, widely employed, but not yet universal). However, there are a number of international signs that have begun to be routinely borrowed by other sign languages. Proper names of countries are a prime example. Signers from each country have a sign for their own country that is distinct from the signs used elsewhere in the world. These native signs are viewed as preferable (and often more culturally acceptable and politically correct) by many signers, and they are gradually moving into general, international use. At the present time, however, the use of these and other international signs is mixed at best and unpredictable from locale to locale. The signs for country names that you will encounter in upcoming pages are primarily ASL, though some are, strictly speaking, the international signs that actually have replaced the ASL signs almost everywhere. In general, today, international signs — those originating from the country in question — are used almost as much as traditional ASL signs for country names.

Nouns

People

People
Move both "P" hands, palm down, in alternating circles at lower torso

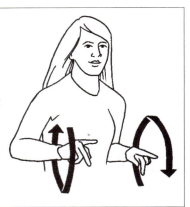

Person
Move both "P" hands, parallel, pointing out, straight down

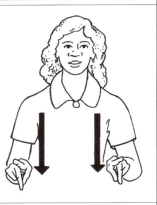

Woman
"5" hand ("A" shape also okay) starts open, thumb to chin, arcs down, and thumb taps sternum

Girl
Right hand "A"; slide thumb tip down jawline almost to chin twice

Man
Right hand "A" ("5" shape also okay) starts with thumb on forehead and moves down into open "5" at midtorso

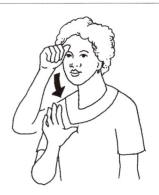

Boy
Right hand flattened "O" shape with palm down; pinch thumb and fingertips twice

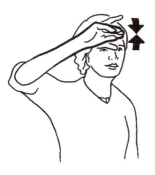

Children
Start palms flat, turned down; move out with gentle bounces (may use one hand or two)

Child

Short, downward movements, indicating a small child's height

Baby

Cradle arms together and swing (rock) gently back and forth twice

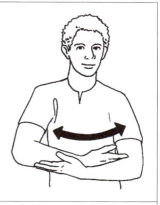

Family

Start with both "F" hands, palms facing; circle out and around until palms face up and little fingers touch

Wife

Thumb of right "claw" hand moves from chin down to clasp palms with left hand

Mother

Right hand "5"; tap thumb on chin, palm facing left — *Note:* fingers in bent "B" postion to form alternate sign for "Grandmother"

Husband

Move right hand "claw" from forehead into clasp with left hand

Father

Right hand "5"; tap thumb against forehead, twice — *Note:* with fingers bent over, this sign becomes an alternate one for "Grandfather"

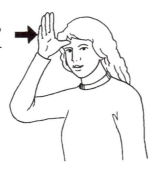

Parents

Right hand "P" starts with middle finger at forehead, then chin (or, sign "Mother/Father" repeatedly)

Stepmother

Right hand "L" pivots from palm in to palm out on angled forearm ("second"); then right hand "5" moves up, thumb to chin, palm left ("mother") — *Note:* may also fingerspell "S T E P"

Stepfather

Right hand "L" pivots from palm in to palm out on angled forearm ("second"); then right hand "5" moves up, thumb to forehead, palm left ("father") — *Note:* may also fingerspell "S T E P"

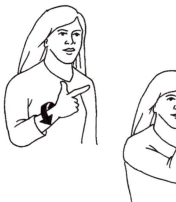

Son

Right hand "B" from visor position on forehead, goes down into still cradle formed by left arm

Daughter

Right hand "A" moves smoothly from right side of chin down to the inside of bent left arm

Sister

Right hand "A" follows jawline and moves down, opening to "L" shape and ends resting on left hand

Brother

Right hand "A" shape over center of forehead; bring down, changing to "L," to rest on back of left "L" hand

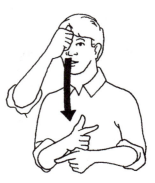

Grandmother

With open hand, touch right thumb to chin; move away from face in two arcs; make same movements and handshape with left hand, but lower

Grandfather

With open hand, touch right thumb to forehead; move away from face in two arcs; make same movements and handshape with left hand, but lower

Uncle

Circle right hand "U" twice near temple

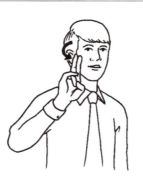

Aunt

With right hand "A," make small circle from above the jawline to below the chin

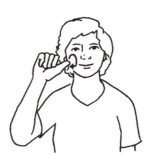

Cousin

Face palm of right hand "C" toward the cheek; twist wrist to show palm, and repeat — *Note:* sign near forehead for male cousin, near chin for female

Niece

Twist right hand "N" near cheek, out and in twice

Nephew

Start right hand "N" palm toward temple, twist in and back twice

Relationship

Both hands "F"; hook right and left thumb/index fingers together; move in and out from body two times

Friend

Both "X" hands; hook right over left, then reverse

Stranger

Right hand "C" arcs right to left in front of face; add person marker

Neighbor

Right hand starts pressed to back of left hand, thumb up; then arcs slightly out; add person marker

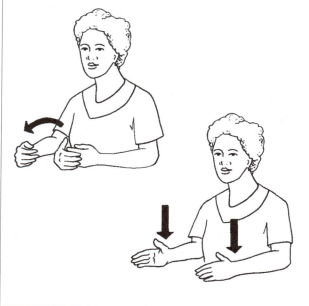

Hypocrite

Closed right hand "5" covers back of closed left hand "5," then right bends left fingers down

Devil

Both hands "3," thumbs at temples, close into claw "3" shapes — *Note:* may use just one hand

Ghost

Start both "F" hands ("8" also okay) with fingers touching, pull right hand up in slightly wavy motion

Angel

Press fingers of bent right hand "B" to shoulder — *Note:* two hands may also be used

Saint

Move heel of right hand "S" from heel over fingers of upturned left hand and make small loop

Robe

"R" hands start palms in near collarbone; move them down and closer together, as in putting on robe

Clothes

Start open hands up at about collarbone height, brush down front of chest two times

Coat

"A" hands move down in arc from shoulder to waist, as in pulling on cloak

Skirt

Brush open hands from waist height down and out twice

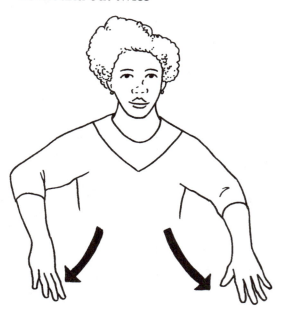

Shirt

With "F" hands, grasp clothing just below collarbone and tug outward twice — *Note:* may use one hand or both

Shoes

Start "S" hands out, tap them together twice

Socks

Rub sides of index fingers together, alternating in and out

Button

Place small-circle right hand "F" at center chest, then at lower chest; may repeat in other positions (collar, cuff) to show number and position of buttons

Belt

Start "B" hands palms in at waist, slightly apart; slide together, interlocking fingers and thumbs

Jewelry

"5" hands start palms in at upper chest and rise slightly; then right middle finger and thumb grasp left wrist, showing jewelry at various positions

Zipper

This modified sign will not always be signed as shown here. Where it is signed (its location in relation to the body) will depend on the location of the zipper being described, which might be a man's fly or a ladies handbag

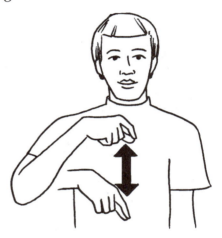

Ring

Move index finger and thumb of right "G" hand up and down the left ring finger

Body, Health, Sickness, and Hygiene

Life

Start "L" handshapes pointing inward at lower torso, then move up to midchest

Death

Start with right hand palm down; left hand up; flip both hands over

Birth

With cupped hands together, palms in, stomach level, move hands out and away in small arc

Health

Touch open hands to shoulders; pull down and away, closing fingers to "S" shape

Sickness

Both "sensing" hands, middle finger of right taps forehead, middle finger of left taps abdomen; *also* "Illness," "Sick"

Cold

Bend right "G" hand near nose with fingers and thumb held apart; move down repeatedly while closing thumb and fingers

Pain

Palms to chest, right slightlyfarther from body than left, bring index fingers almost together repeatedly— *Note:* locate sign where pain is

Blood

Right hand palm in, start index finger across both lips, then crook ("red"); then wriggle right "5" hand, crossed over left hand in front of chest, and move it down

Medicine

With middle finger of right hand "5" bent and other fingers spread out, rub middle finger side to side on palm of left hand

Menstruation

Right hand "A" palm toward cheek taps the cheek twice

Birth Control

Sign "baby": left hand cradles right, palms up, rocking; then sign "prevent": left hand palm angled down and toward body; right hand moves firmly between left thumb and index — *Note:* also commonly fingerspelled "B C"

Abortion

Start left hand closed "5," right hand claw "C"; bring right hand down, closing into "S"; then out, opening into "5"

Sex (intercourse)

Both "V" hands, right palm down, left palm up, tap together twice

Nurse

Right "N" fingertips touch left wrist twice

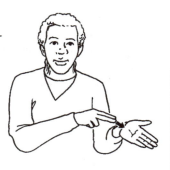

Doctor

Right hand "M"(or "D") on upturned left wrist (at pulse)

Psychiatrist

Tap right midfinger of right hand "P" on upturned left wrist

Accident

Start with "5" fingers open and slightly curved; close fingers as hands move together

Soap

Touch right flat fingertips to left palm; pull outside, closing, repeat movement twice

Bath
Hands "scrubbing" up and down repeatedly along front of body

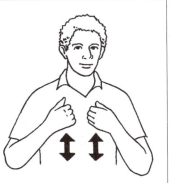

Toothbrush
Draw "1" finger back and forth in front of mouth, wriggling up and down

Rough Sex, Rape
Both "S" hands; forcefully tap heel of right against inside of left wrist

Body
Place open palms on upper torso; move down and place on lower torso

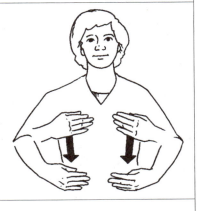

Brain
Index finger to right temple — *also* "Mind," "Think" (for verb, add circular movement with index finger)

Head
With bent open right hand, touch temple, then lower jaw

Hair
With right hand "F" hold and shake a bit of hair

Face
Right hand circles face clockwise

Mirror
Closed "5" hand, fingers up, pivots at wrist, moving palm from facing in to facing out

Eye
Point right hand "1" at right eye; for plural (eyes), point at right then left, below and in front of eyes

Glasses
Both hands "G" at temples; hands mimic following arms of glasses back twice — *Note:* may sign with just one hand

Contact lenses
Open "5" hand with middle finger bent inward; tap just over each eye (without touching) as if putting in/taking out lenses — *Note:* also common to fingerspell "C L"

Ear
Pinch and pull ear lobe

Nose
Right hand "1" touching nose

Mouth
With palm to face, circle mouth with right index finger

Voice
Arc "V" fingers forward from throat

Back

Tap back of right shoulder twice with downturned fingertips

Heart

Middle fingers of both sensing hands together draw a heart shape over the heart

Heart

Touch middle finger of right hand "5" to center of chest — *Note:* this is the "feeling" handshape

Arm

Both hands open and bent; move right hand down the left arm

Stomach

Fingers of right hand bent "B" tap just above waist twice

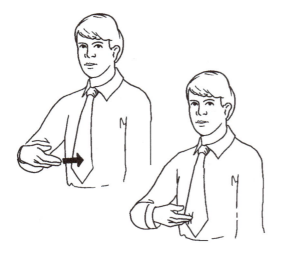

Hands

Right hand slices across thumb side of left, then left does same to right; hands at right angles both times

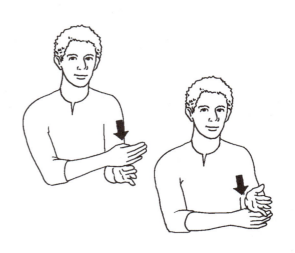

Leg

Tap right thigh
with right hand;
also common to
fingerspell

Finger

Touch left fingers
one by one with
extended right
index finger

Toes

Point with right hand to feet, then with
right hand point to fingers of left hand

Feet

Point down to left,
then right foot with
right hand

Work, Study, Art, and Money

School

Clap right hand twice, crosswise on left palm

Principal

Right hand "P" circles middle finger clockwise over top of left hand; ends touching top of left hand with middle finger

Class

Both "C" hands rotate from wrists down and together

Teacher

"O" hands start at temples and move out; then add person marker

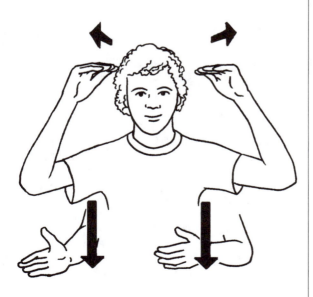

Student

Right hand claw "5" starts with fingers pressed to left palm, pulls away and to the right with fingers closing; add person marker

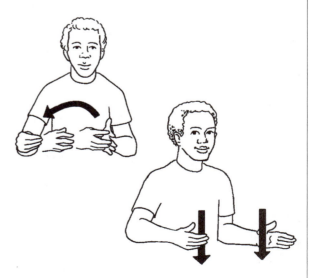

Lesson

Little finger edge of right hand bent "B" touches fingertips and then palm of left hand

Vocabulary

Palm "V" fingers at angle on left index finger

Dictionary

Right hand "D" moves in circle over open left palm (as in thumbing pages); and repeats

Page

Draw right hand "A" along open left palm, as if thumbing through pages

Paper

Both hands open, palms facing together, fingers in opposite directions; right hand pulls across heel of left, twice

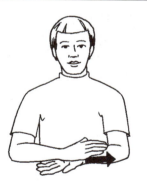

Pencil

Tips of bent right thumb and index finger, palm in, touch mouth; right hand then moves down across open left hand, from heel to end of fingertips

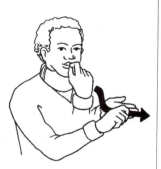

Word

Right hand "G" taps twice against upturned index finger of left hand "1"

Fingerspelling

Open right hand at shoulder height, palm down; wriggle fingers and move back and forth

Sign

With index fingers up, alternate circling hands toward body — *also* used as verb

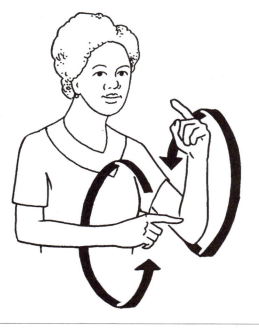

Preschool

Left hand bent "B" curved around back of right hand "P"; then palms of both bent "B" hands press together ("School")

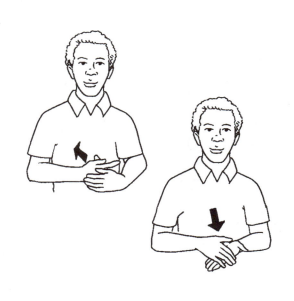

Kindergarten

Right hand "K," left hand closed "5"; right hand rocks back and forth under the left palm

Elementary School

Right hand "S," palm out, rocks back and forth under palm of flat left hand

High School

Fingerspell "H" and "S"

Oral School

Right hand "O" makes small circle in front of mouth

Middle School

Flat right hand "B" circles, then bends and presses fingers down onto left palm, then presses right palm to left palm

Residential School for the Deaf

Right index finger touches near ear, then chin ("Deaf"); then little finger side of right "I" taps left "I" thumb joint twice

Mainstream School

Both "5" hands start at upper chest, flow together, then right palm claps left palm twice

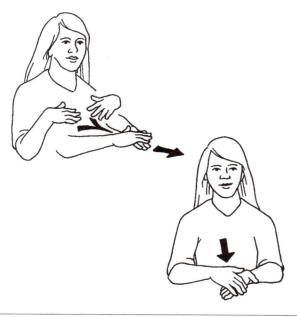

Public (Hearing) School

Right index finger starts at lips and makes small outward circle, then right palm claps left palm twice

Science

Both "A" hands, knuckles facing knuckles, move in alternating circles

Music

Swing "M" hand back and forth above extended left arm (left palm facing right)

Art

Move right little finger against palm in an "S" curve as hand comes down — *also* "Artist," but must add person marker

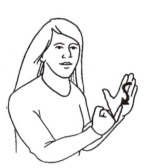

Poetry

Swing "P" hand back and forth over left arm

Writer

Close the index finger and thumb of right hand "T/X" and "scribble" on open left palm; add person marker

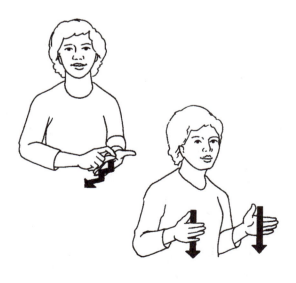

Picture

Right hand "C" moves palm out from temple, then down, ending with right thumb and index finger side of hand on left palm, left fingers up

Newspaper

Right hand "G" on base of left palm, open and close thumb and index finger several times

Magazine

Fingers of right hand "G," palm facing body, moves from fingertips of left hand to heel, twice

Story (generic; a string of sentences)

Both "F" hands start at midchest, fingers touching, with right palm facing out and left palm facing in; hands move out, come together as before but switching palm orientation, and move out again. With an "8" handshape, sign means to tell a tale; with a bent "B," it means to weave a long and involved story.

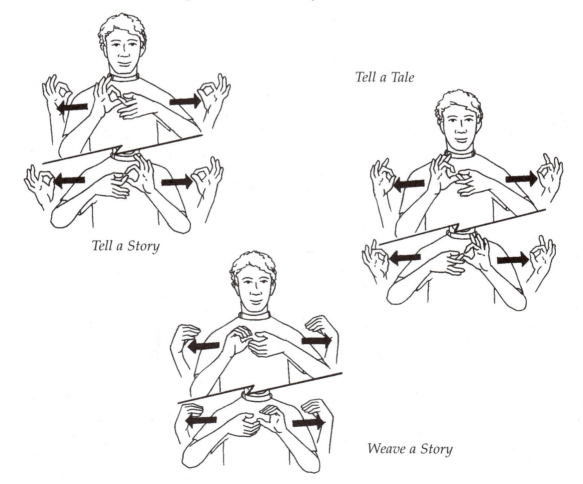

Tell a Story

Tell a Tale

Weave a Story

Book

Palms together, then open with small fingers touching; repeat — *also* as verb, to open a book: show single movement of opening; to close a book: show single movement of closing

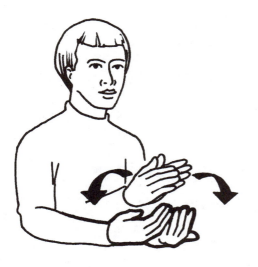

Job

Both "S" hands; tap bottom of right wrist against back of left wrist — *also* "Work"

Promotion

Move both bent "B" (or bent, closed "5") hands from shoulder height to head height

Office

Start both "O" hands, left in front of right; pull hands apart, move right straight out, left straight back, describing square dimensions

Employee

Tap wrist of palm-down, right hand "A" on back of left hand "A"; add person marker — *also* "Worker"

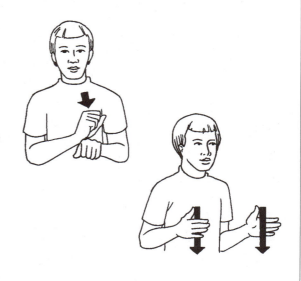

Appointment

Right hand starts as "claw," circles clockwise over top of left hand and closes to "S" shape resting on back of left hand

Department

Start with both "D" hands, palms facing; circle out and around until palms face up and little fingers touch

Project

Move fingertips of right hand "P" up length of left palm and fingers, then change to "J" shape and move down to base of left hand and back up

Meeting

Start closed "5" hands palms facing together, slighty apart in front of upper chest; fold together in bent "B" shapes with right over left

Computer

Right hand "C" begins on back of palm-down left hand, moves right to left in arc

Schedule

Open right hand faces out; left hand faces in; right fingers touch left palm, moving down, then palm turns inward and pulls sideways, describing a graph — *Note:* same for noun and verb

Advertisement

Start right hand in "C" shape under left fist; move down, away from left, into "S" shape, repeatedly

Phone

"Y" hand; thumb to ear, little finger to chin; tap knuckles on cheek twice — *Note:* to sign the verb, tap only once, or pull away once

Stamp
Right hand "H" fingers tap lips, then press down on left fingertips

Letter
Move right thumb from lips down to left fingertips, as if applying stamp to envelope

Tape
Draw right hand "H" down and across fingers of left hand "H"

Machine
Both claw "4" hands loosely interweave knuckles; move hands up and down several times, as in rolling gears

Equipment
Start right hand "E" palm up, move right in small arcs

Wood
Little finger side of right hand "B" saws back and forth across back of left hand

Glass
Right hand "X" index finger taps teeth twice

Rubber
Right "X" index finger taps the right cheek, moving down, twice

Key
Right hand "X,"
twist knuckle in
left palm

Rope
"R" fingers
start
together;
move out
in spirals

Lock
Start left hand "S" and right hand in
claw "5," palm out near shoulder; circle
and close right hand into "S" shape,
palm up, and press backs of hands
together

Thread
Both "I" hands, palms to body; little
fingers together, right and left hands
spiral out in opposite directions

Sack
Start loose "claw"
hands, palms fac-
ing up, little fin-
gers touching; arc
apart and up until
palms face together
— *also* "Bag"

Box
Flat hands
describe first the
front and back
(with right hand
nearer the body),
then sides — *also*
"Room," "Office"
(with "O" hands)

Dollar

Clasp right hand firmly on left fingers, then slide across and out

Cents

Draw right index finger out several inches from right temple

Coins

Draw circles with right finger in left palm

Check

Both hands with index finger and thumb in "C" shape, other fingers in fist, forming rectangle in front of face; then move out to sides as index fingers curl down to thumbs

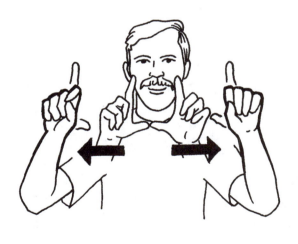

Money

Tap back of fingers of right flattened "O" hand to upturned left palm twice

Price

Right hand "X": bring midsection of index finger down across open left palm, twice

Profit

Move right hand "F" from in front of torso into imaginary shirt pocket, twice — *also* "Benefit"

Reward

Both "X" hands, right closer to chest than left, move outward in simultaneous arcs, palms facing — *also* "Prize"

Tax

Bring right finger "X" across open left palm — *also* "Cost," but only do once

Judge

Both "F" hands, palms facing together, alternate moving up and down; add person marker

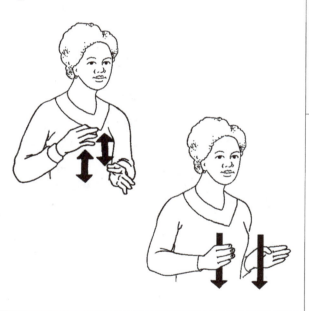

Debt

Right index finger taps left palm, which faces right (may also face up)

Attorney

Right hand "L" palm facing left; touch fingers, then palm of left hand ("Law"); plus person marker — *also* "Lawyer"

Expert

Start with "F" hand on chin, palm facing left; twist to palm down

Secretary

Right hand "H" moves from side of face near right ear and down, then fingers stroke out along left palm

Manager

Both "T/X" hands with palms facing; first move in toward body and out, then add person marker

Preacher

Start "F" hand at side of face palm out, bend forward at wrist repeatedly; then move both hands parallel, palms facing, down side of body (person marker)

Accountant

Right hand "F" fingers move twice from heel to fingers of left hand; followed by person marker

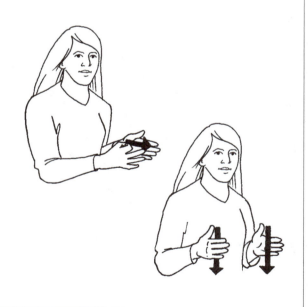

President

"C" hands at temples; slowly move out and close into "S" hands — *also* "Superintendent"

Baby-sitter
Make sign for "Baby" plus sign for "Take Care" and add person marker

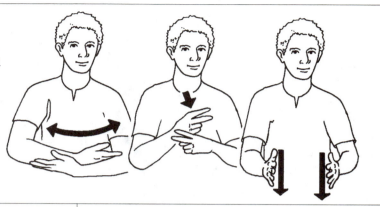

Inspector
Right index finger starts at eye, goes to left palm, then out ("Look" or "Inspect"); plus person marker

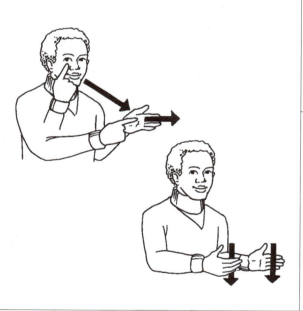

King
Draw "K" hand from left shoulder area to right waist — *also* "Queen" (but use "Q" handshape), "Christ" (with "C" hand), "Prince" ("P" hand), and "Lord" ("L" hand)

Queen
Draw "Q" hand from left shoulder area to right waist — *also* "King" (but use "K" handshape), "Christ" (with "C" hand), "Prince" ("P" hand) and "Lord" ("L" hand)

Government
Right index finger circles, crooks into "X" shape, then points to temple with palm down

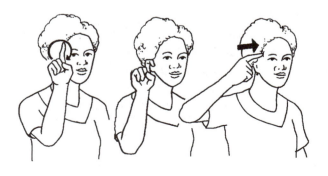

Police

Place "C" hand just below left shoulder and tap twice (a badge)

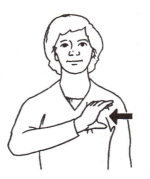

Army

Tap both "A" hands against chest twice — *also* "Soldier," but add person marker

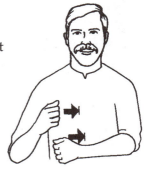

Soldier

Tap both "A" hands against chest twice ("Army"); add person marker

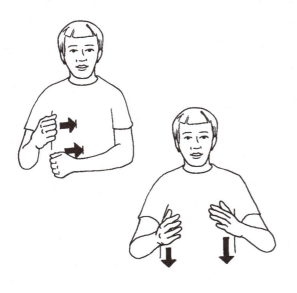

Enemy

Horizontal index fingers start together, pull apart; add person marker

Officer

Tap claw "5/C" right hand on right shoulder twice — *also* "Boss" or "Coach"

War

Both "5" hands, with wriggling fingers, arc back and forth from left to right, remaining equidistant

Play, Leisure, and Travel

Fun
Both "U" hands; bring right fingers from nose down, touch left fingers (frequently fingerspelled)

Holiday
Both "5" hands, double-tap thumbs to armpits

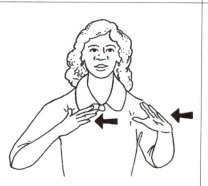

Christmas
Start right hand "C" palm down; flip, moving arm right, to palm up, from shoulder to shoulder

Thanksgiving
Start right "O" at mouth, with both palms facing body, move hands up, opening fingers as they rise

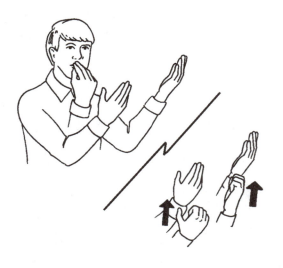

Wedding
Flat open hands start apart, palms down, then sweep together, right hand clasping atop left

Anniversary
Both "T/X" hands make tight circles in and out

Party
Both "P" hands swing loosely from side to side

Bar
Thumb of right and left "A" hands alternate in and out at mouth, palms angled partly out

Movie
Right hand "5" with heel on open left hand; twist back and forth

Play (drama)
Both "A" hands, thumbs toward body, move in alternating circles toward chest

Applause
Raised "5" hands lifted above shoulders and shaken rapidly, palms out

Television
Fingerspell "T" and "V"; repeat quickly

Radio
Curl claw "5" hand over ear and rotate wrist in and out — *Note:* may use both hands

Ticket
Move right, bent double "X" fingers near left little fingers with left palm up, twice

Trip
Move bent fingers of right hand "V" in small waves, right to left

Train
Right "H" fingers move back and forth twice on back of left "H" fingers

Automobile
Turn imaginary steering wheel twice — *also* "Car"

Airplane
Move "I Love You" hand (palm down) up, out, and slightly away; twice — *also* "Fly" (verb, in an airplane), but move hand farther out and only once

Ship
With right hand "3" resting on left palm, move both hands forward in little waves

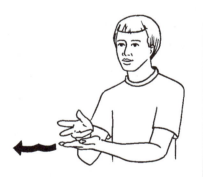

Boat
Cup hands, pressing little fingers together; move forward in wavy motion

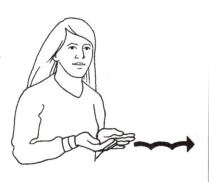

Bicycle
"S" hands mimic the motion of feet on pedals

Ball

Enclose round space with claw "C" hands; tap fingertips together several times

Doll

Stroke right "X" index finger up and down twice on length of bridge of nose — *also* "Pretend"

Skateboard

Right index and middle fingers touch left ones, move outward in wavy motion

Game

Both "A" hands with thumbs up, palms facing body, tap together twice at knuckles

Roller skates

Both hands in upturned bent double "X" shapes; arms move back and forth alternately — *also* "Skating," "Ice skates"

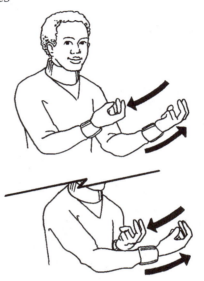

Basketball

Open curved hands, as if holding a ball; then toss/release motion (as in player making a two-handed pass)

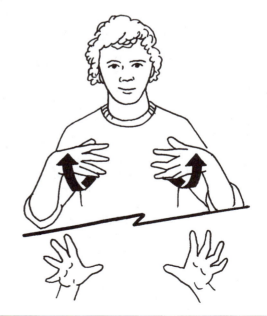

Team

Both "T" hands start with index fingers touching, palms out; circle out and around until little fingers touch, palms in

Football

"5" hands facing each other, move together, interlace fingers; repeat several times

Baseball

Both "S" hands mimic grasping a bat and swinging it, twice

Volleyball

Flick open hands forward twice from face height

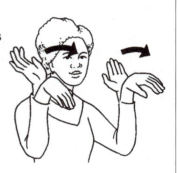

Tennis

Start right hand "A" up at right shoulder, swing down and left; then start at left shoulder, swing down and right

Bowling

Curved, open fingers as if grasping ball; then arc forward (as if releasing ball)

Billiards

With right hand in cue-holding position, "strike" toward left hand "F" — *also* "To shoot pool"

Food and Eating

Breakfast

First sign "Eat": tap lips twice with flattened "O" hand; then "Morning": put left fingers inside crook of right arm and move right arm upward with palm up

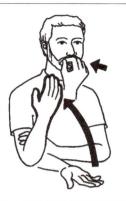

Lunch

With right hand "L" pointing up, thumb taps bottom of chin, twice

Dinner

Fingers/thumb of right hand touch mouth ("Eat"); then bent open right hand touches back of left wrist ("Night")

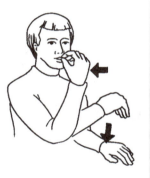

Dessert

Tap fingers of "D" hands together, several times

Plate

Both index fingers and thumbs forming "C" hands, with palms in, indicating plate shape

Bowl

Cup hands, little fingers together, then pull out and up, opening into "C" hands

Cup

Move right hand "C" down into flat left palm twice

Glass

Start right hand "C" in left palm; move up a few inches

Spoon

Scoop twice with right "U" fingers from left palm to mouth — *also* "Soup"

Fork

Right hand "V" spears open left palm twice, facing right

Knife

Both "1" hands; pointing right index finger left, scrape down left index finger several times in whittling motion

Napkin

Tap open right fingers (flattened "O" hand also okay) across lips from right to left

Food

Right hand thumb and fingers together, repeatedly move in short motions toward mouth — *also* "Eat," but only do once

Bread

Right hand claw "5" slices repeatedly with fingertips against backs of left fingers (left hand can be closed "5" or "B")

Cracker

Tap right hand "A" above left elbow

Toast

Touch "V" right fingers to back of left hand; then flip left hand and touch palm

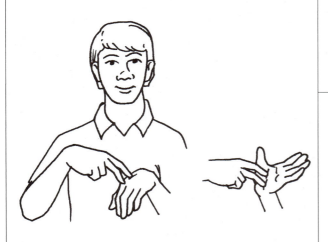

Butter

Press right hand "U" fingers along length of upturned palm

Grease

Right thumb and middle finger grasp little finger side of left, palm-inward, hand; right hand pulls down from left as it closes

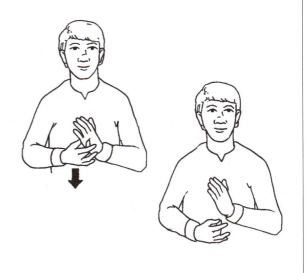

Cheese

"Grind" heel of right hand "S" on palm of upturned left hand, fingers pointing in opposite directions

Fish

Both "B" hands; left fingertips touching right wrist; glide hands out, wriggling right fingertips

Meat

With right thumb and index finger, pinch flesh of left hand between thumb and index finger

Chicken
Right hand "G," open/close thumb and index finger several times — *also* "Bird"

Egg
Both "H" hands; strike right fingers against left, then sweep down and apart, twice — *also* as verb (to crack an egg), but just do once

Salt
Both "V" hands alternately tap right index and middle fingers up and down over left middle and index fingers

Pepper
Shake right hand "F" down slightly at wrist, twice

Fruit
Right hand "F"; twist forward repeatedly at side of mouth

Pear
Left hand, fingers and thumb together, palm in; right hand starts with fingers over left fingertips, pulls out and closes to flattened "O"

Orange
Start claw "5" hand in front of lower face; close into "S" hand, twice

Grapes

Tap right-hand fingers from knuckles and up back of left hand

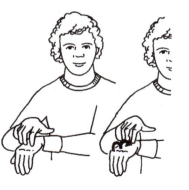

Banana

Motion of banana peeling; left index finger is banana

Melon

Right middle finger flicks away from thumb, then thumps back of left hand, twice — *also* "Pumpkin"

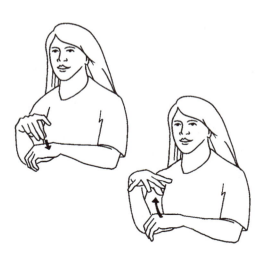

Lemon

Right hand "L" with thumb to chin and index finger pointing up; twist to left so palm turns down — *Note:* "L" plus "Sour"

Apple

Twist "X" hand, palm in/palm out several times

Vegetable

With "V" index finger on chin, palm out, rotate wrist and flip hands so middle finger is on chin and palm is facing in

Salad

Start both claw "C" hands, palms facing up; arc up in tossing motion

Beans

Both hands open "G," fingers touch; move out from body, separating hands slightly and closing fingers

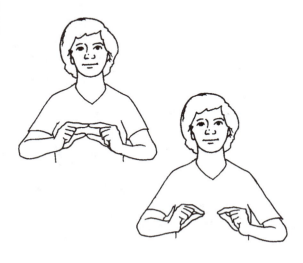

Tomato

Right "1" moves down from mouth, "slicing" the tomato shape formed by the left "O" hand

Onion

Curved "X" hand twists twice at corner of eye

Corn

Both "A" hands, knuckles out, twist hands forward and back at wrist (gnawing the cob)

Cabbage

Tap heel of right hand at right temple

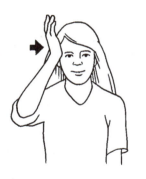

Potato

Tap right, bent "V" fingers on top of left hand

Spaghetti

Start little fingers of "I" hands touching; pull hands apart and up in small arcs — *also* "Pasta"

Soup

Arc right "H" fingers from chest down into left palm, then up and out

Sugar

Brush right closed "5" hand down from chin and into "A," twice — *Note:* same for "Sweet," but do only once

Candy

Brush right index finger down chin from right corner and then left corner of mouth

Gum

Right bent "V" hand bends repeatedly on right cheek, keeping fingertips near right corner of mouth

Chocolate

Hold right hand "C" on the back of the palm-down left hand and move in circle

Cookie

Touch right fingertips to left palm; twist hands in opposite directions

Ice cream

Right hand "S" moves in toward body in a circular motion, twice (eating ice cream)

Pie

With thumb up, palm left, slide right hand on left palm; repeat at two different angles (slicing pie)

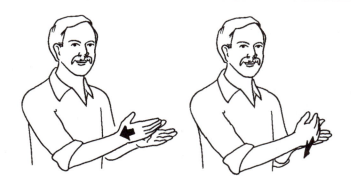

Cake

Place fingertips of claw "C" right hand in open left palm; circle right hand repeatedly

Jelly

Flick right hand "J" several times on left palm, as if spreading jam

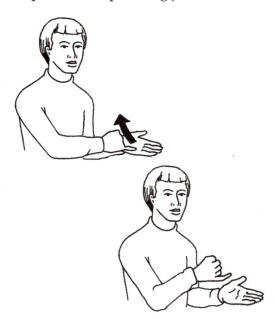

Drink

Start with right hand "C," palm left, thumb touching just below lip and tip toward mouth twice — *also*, as verb, but just do once

Water

Tap right hand "W" twice to lower lip

Milk

Right hand claw "C" squeezes to "S" and open, twice

Soft drink

Insert index finger and thumb of the right hand "F" down into the opening of the left hand "O," then slap down

Coke

Poke index finger of right hand "L" into upper arm; poke twice. This is a very regional (Southern) sign; most ASL signers elsewhere finger-spell it

Tea

Right hand "F" makes stirring/dipping movement into left hand "O," twice

Coffee

Both "S" hands, palms toward body, move in circular, grinding motion

Beer

Right hand "B," index finger near mouth; draw hand in a circular movement several times

Whiskey

With index and little fingers of each hand extended, tap right hand twice against top of left

Wine

Circle right "W" fingers on right cheek several times

Places and Furnishings

Universe
"U" hands circle each other

Star
Palms out, fingertips up, brush index fingers back and forth

Planet
Left hand "S" (Sun); right hand "P"; right hand starts near body and circles left completely

Moon
Curve right index finger and thumb around eye, then move right hand up and out

World
Both "W" hands; right hand circles out and away from body and back around, resting on left hand

Earth
Left hand "S"; thumb and middle finger of right hand grasp left hand across knuckles and rock back and forth (as if on axis)

Geography
Both "G" hands; right hand circles out and away from body and back around, resting on left hand

Sky

Both bent "B" hands, palms down, start above forehead, right slightly lower; right circles completely around left hand, then both hands come down and out

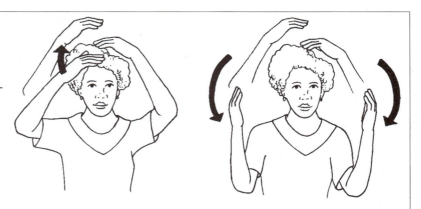

Ocean

Right hand "W," index finger to chin; move both hands flat, open, and palms out, away from body in wavy motion (right hand stays closer to body)

Mountain

Start with both "S" hands, then tap right hand on back of left; open hands and move up in wavy motion, left hand higher

Hills

Both hands open and angled, right hand lower, move up in a wavy motion

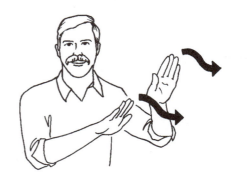

Beach

Both "5" hands with forearms parallel to ground; right hand moves left in waves above back of left hand and arm

River

Tap index finger of right hand "W" on chin; then push both open hands, palms facing, in forward, curvy line

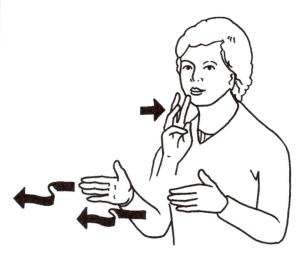

Land

With both hands, rub thumbs against fingers, turn hands down and open, then circle inward once and stop — *Note:* may be signed with one or both hands

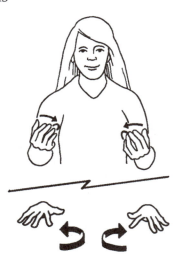

Country

Right open hand, fingertips rub left elbow; left palm facing in, toward body

Island

Side of right hand below the little finger moves in circle on back of left hand

Nation

Right hand "N" circles clockwise above back of left hand

Africa

Right "5" hand, palm out, starts shoulder height, moves right, then down, changing into flattened "O" — *also* "African"

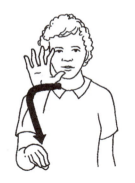

America

Interlock fingers, circle hands together from left to right (all together in a melting pot) — *also* "American"

Asia

Start with thumb of right hand "A" to corner of eye, palm up; pivot forward and down — *also* "Asian"

Australia

Touch fingertips of right, open hand to forehead, then flip hand palm out, thumb in — *also* "Australian"

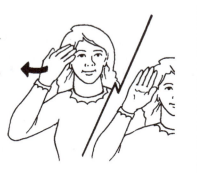

Canada

Right hand "A" pulls/returns right side of "lapel," twice — *also* "Canadian"

China

Extended right index finger, palm in, draws line across collarbone, then straight down, turning palm and index finger upward — *also* "Chinese"

England

Cross right hand over back of left, with fingers of right hand curled under — *also* "English"

Europe

Right hand "E," with palm facing body, circles at forehead, then rests on forehead

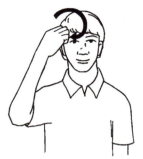

France

"F" hand with palm facing out; rotate wrist until palm faces body — *also* "French"

Germany

Both "5" hands, left thumb and index finger clasp right wrist as all fingers wriggle — *also* "German"

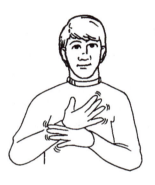

Japan

Both "G" hands start close together at midabdomen, then arc out slightly, fingers closing

India

Start thumb of "A" hand on forehead, tap twice on forehead — *also* "Indian" (not "Native American")

South America

Right hand "S," palm out, moves from upper chest straight down ("South"); then loosely twine fingers of hands and move together in circle at midtorso ("America") — *also* "South American"

Spain

Start hands palm in, "X" handshapes; bring hands down together, hooking right index over left index finger — *also* "Spanish"

United States

Fingerspell "U" and "S" — *Note:* may also use as adjective

Washington, DC

Circle "W" hand at right shoulder; then fingerspell "D" and "C"

Highway

Start with both "U" hands near shoulders, palms facing each other; move right hand forward, left hand back, bending into "N" shape

Road

Move "B" hands, palms facing, out from body

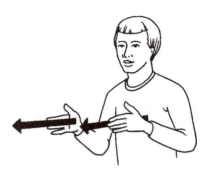

Town

Bring open fingertips together at angle repeatedly, moving arms left each time (many houses) — *also* "City," "Village"

Bridge

Touch right hand "V" fingertips to left palm; then swing "V" hand to inside crook of left arm

Farm

Right hand "5" taps below left corner of mouth, then below right corner of mouth

Building

Stack one hand atop the other, rising, alternating repeatedly

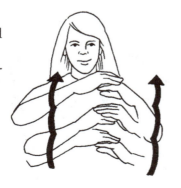

Church

Tap back of right hand "C" thumb on back of left hand "S" (or "B")

Temple
Heel of right hand "T" taps back of left hand

College
Flat right hand with palm facing left palm; circles and slides up and out while palm remains facing down

Neighborhood
Start right closed "5" hand clasped to back of similar left hand; then circle flat right hand from right, forward, and around above left hand — *also* "Town"

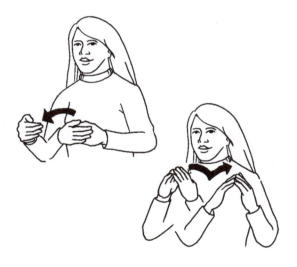

Address
Move "A" hands, thumbs up, upward in unison

Store
Start with "O" hands at shoulder level, rotate wrists out twice

Library
Move right hand "L" in circle to right at about shoulder height

Hospital
Right hand "H"; with fingertips, draw letter "X" on sleeve

Pharmacy
Press middle finger of open right hand to left palm and rock back and forth ("Medicine"); then swing both flattened "O" hands from palm facing in to palm facing down ("Store") — *Note:* substitute person marker for store to form "Pharmacist"

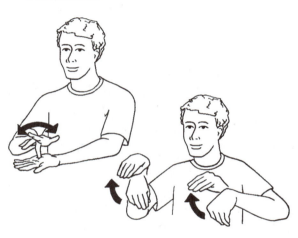

Jail
Both hands "4"; bring together repeatedly with back of right against left palm

Restaurant
Right hand "R" touches face near corner of mouth; moves down, then left — *also* "Cafeteria" with "C" handshape

House
"B" hands start at face, go down and out at angle, then down

Home
With right fingers and thumb together, touch below lower lip, then upper cheekbone

Hallway
Both hands closed "5" straight up, palms facing, move straight out, staying equidistant

Room

Start both "B" hands, left in front of right; pull hands apart, move right straight out, left straight back, describing square dimensions

Kitchen

Flip right hand "K" from palm down to palm up, on left palm, twice

Restroom

Bounce right hand "R" down with palm down, then out from body

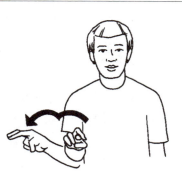

Floor

Both "B" hands start touching at thumbs; slide smoothly out

Wall

Face "B" palms out; pull smoothly, straight out to sides

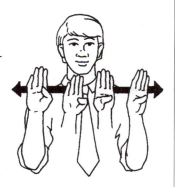

Ceiling

Both flat hands start side by side over the head, right hand in front; slide right forward without lowering it

Door

Both "B" hands, side by side, "hinged" at little finger sides; pull right hand back in arc, twice — *also,* as verb (to open/close door), but just do once

Window

Both "B" hands, palms face body, right taps down on left twice

Stairs

Move "B" hands in alternating "steps" upward

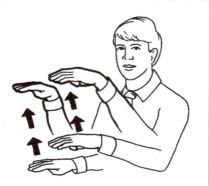

Elevator

Move right hand "E" up and down against left palm twice

Bed

Tilt head with right palm to right cheek

Table

With both closed "5" hands, bring right arm and palm flat down atop left, twice

Chair

Right "U" fingers curve over flat left "U" fingers, palms down, tap twice — *also* "Sit," but for verb use single movement

Sofa

Tap right hand "U" onto left hand "U" ("Chair"); then bring "C" hands, palms down, together at waist and out ("Length")

Bedroom

"Bed": press right hand to right cheek, tilt head; "Room": bent, closed "5" hands several inches apart (showing front and back walls), then palms facing together (side walls)

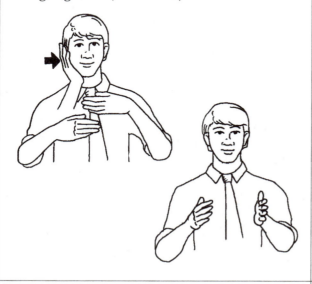

Dining Room

Touch thumb and fingers to lips ("Eat"); bent, closed "5" hands several inches apart (front and back walls), then palms facing together (side walls)

Time and Climate

Time

Double-tap right index finger to back of left wrist

Clock

Right hand "1" taps back of left hand "S"; then both hands rise to "C," thumbs and fingertips touching

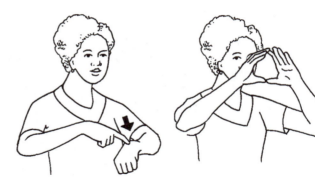

Minute

Right hand "1," knuckles on left palm; right index finger starts pointing up, then hand twists, dragging right index finger from thumb, across left fingers (minute hand on face of clock)

Hour

Circle right index finger around; end back with right palm to left palm

Week

With right "1" index finger pointing left, place right hand heel at left hand heel and move across left palm to fingertips

Weekend

Sign "Week"; then bring right hand away from left and slice down

Month

Both hands "1," right palm facing in; point right finger to left and rub down the back of left index finger, left palm facing out

Monday

Right hand "M" circles once clockwise (from signer's perspective)

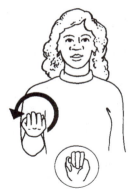

Tuesday

Right hand "T" circles once clockwise (from signer's perspective)

Wednesday
Right hand "W" circles once clockwise (from signer's perspective)

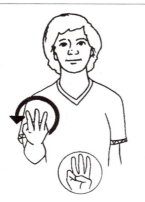

Thursday
Right hand "H" circles once clockwise (from signer's perspective)

Friday
Right hand "F" circles once counter-clockwise (from signer's perspective)

Saturday
Right hand "S" circles once counter-clockwise (from signer's perspective)

Sunday
Palms out, "5" hands both circle out and then in together

Today
Bent "B" hands, palms in, start below shoulders and move straight down ("Now"); start right forearm angled above horizontal left forearm; bring right forearm and flat hand down to meet left ("Today")

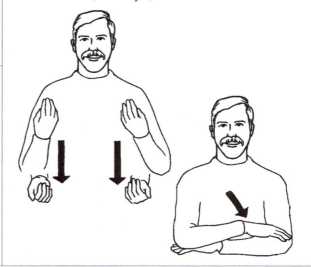

Day
Start with right forearm angled above horizontal left forearm; bring right forearm and flat hand down to meet left

Tonight

Closed, bent "5" hands, palms in, start below shoulders and move straight down ("Now"); bend right hand over back of left wrist ("Night")

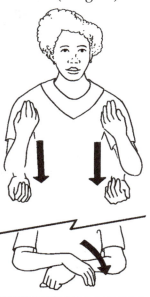

Tomorrow

Start right hand "A" thumbs up at upper jaw with thumb pointing straight back; hand arcs forward just past cheek, ending just in front of face with thumb up

Yesterday

Move right hand "A" thumb out from right corner of mouth to top of jaw

Birthday

Begin right hand with palm to chest ("Happy"); move up and down twice, down to rest on left palm (alternate sign for "Birth")

Sunset

Right, closed "F" hand starts above horizontal left arm, moves in arc downward

Sunrise

Right, closed "F" hand starts slightly below horizontal left arm, moves in arc upward

Morning

Place fingers of open left hand in crook of right arm, palm facing down; gently pull open right palm toward face

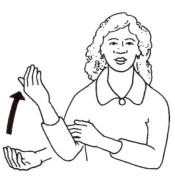

Noon

Right hand "B" straight up, palm left; right elbow on back of left hand, tap twice

Afternoon

Rest right arm at about 45 degree angle, lightly atop back of left hand

Evening

Lay right hand curved over left; tap right wrist several times over back of left hand — *also* "Night"

Midnight

Hold left hand "B" with little finger in crook of right elbow; right hand "B" points down, palm left

Year

Both "S" hands start right resting on left; right circles forward and under left, returning to starting position

Time, Era

Right hand "S" draws, clockwise, a circle on palm of left hand

Spring

Right hand "O" moves up through left hand "C" and opens to "5" shape with short, quick motions, twice

Summer

Drag right index finger "1" from left to right across forehead, closing into "X" shape as it goes

Fall

Brush right hand "4" down left forearm, near elbow — *also* "Autumn"

Winter

Shiver "S" hands tightly back and forth

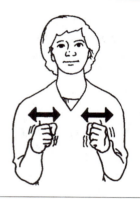

Weather

Both "W" hands; press thumbs together and pivot/twist in alternating movements

Snow

Start right hand open "5" with thumb at upper chest, move out to flattened "O" ("White"); then both "5" hands start near head and wiggle down in wavy motion ("Fluttering down")

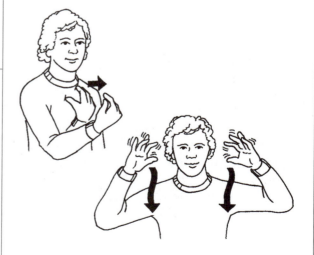

Wind

Both open "5" hands wave back and forth broadly; varies with intensity of wind being described

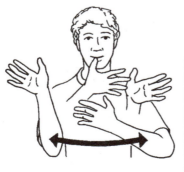

Rain

At shoulder height, repeatedly bend wrists of both claw "5" hands

Storm

Open "5" hands move from right, sweep across front of body, reversing palm positions, repeatedly — *Note:* the vigor of the moment is increased to show a more violent storm

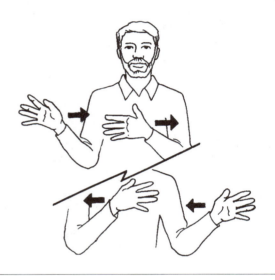

Umbrella

Begin right hand "S" resting on left "S"; raise right, to face level

Cloud

Claw "5" hands; right palm out, left palm in, at forehead height; right hand circles out and right

Flood

"Water" ("W" hand to lips) plus "Rise" (both hands "5," palms down, raised straight up)

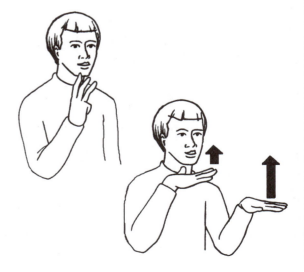

Drought

Draw extended right index finger across chin, from left to right, closing into "X" shape — *also* "Dry"

Sun

"1" hand, palm facing right, circles high, stops with palm out, then changes to flattened "O" and moves down toward right temple with fingers opening

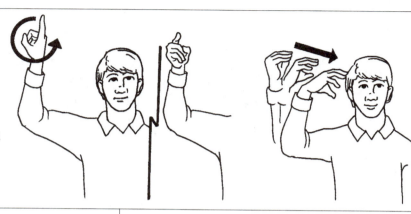

Fire

Both "5" hands; wriggle fingers and move hands, alternating up and down

Electricity

Both "X" hands; strike index fingers together repeatedly — *also*, as verb (flow electrically), but just do once

Shadow

Right hand "5" starts near right temple, palm angled left/down, then moves down in wavy line until fingers are pointing down

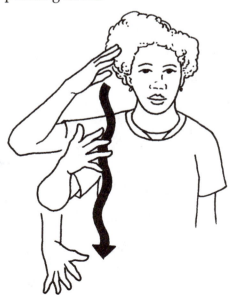

Light

Middle finger and thumb pressed together, middle finger flicks against lips repeatedly

Animals
and
Plants

Animal
Start with palms facing opposite directions, fingertips touching chest below shoulders; roll hands over until their backs face together, keeping finger tips to chest; repeat

Horse
Start with "U" hands, thumbs at temples; roll fingers down — *Note:* may use just one hand

Cow
"Y" hand or hands at forehead to form horns, do once or twice

Fox
Twist "F" hand back and forth in front of nose

Dog
Right hand palm up; snap thumb and index finger twice

Lion

"Claw" moves from forehead over top of head, with palm opening out, as if describing a lion's mane

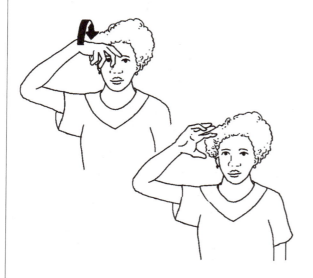

Pig

Bend fingers of closed "5" flat hand twice under chin

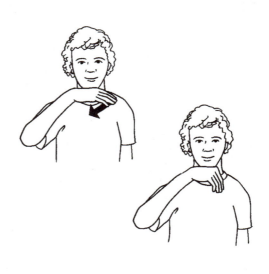

Cat

With "F" hand, stroke imaginary whisker out from side of mouth twice (may move both hands in identical motions)

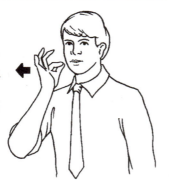

Mouse

Flick extended index finger along nose twice

Rat

Flick "R" fingers across nose twice

Squirrel

Start the right double "X" hand with fingers crooked at side of nose; move down and tap fingertips to those of left double "X" hand

Turkey

"X" or "Q" hand moves from hooked over nose down to tap twice on chest

Bird

Right hand "G"; open and close thumb and index finger several times

Fish

Both "B" hands; left fingertips touching right wrist; move hands out, wriggling right fingertips

Wings

Bent flat fingers point out and flutter, pivoting at wrists, as wings flutter

Elephant

Right "B" hand starts palm out, moves down describing elephant trunk, ends palm down

Snake

Start double "X" right hand fingers at mouth; move forward in brisk, single spiral

Frog

From under chin, flick right index and middle fingers from thumb, against underside of chin

Turtle

Left hand cups thumb side of right hand; right thumb wriggles

Insect

Start thumb of "3" hand on nose; bend middle and index fingers down

Bee

Touch right hand "F" fingers against right cheek, then "slap" cheek (swatting a bee)

Butterfly

Start with hands crossed at wrists, thumbs hooked; flutter finger "wings" inward and upward twice — *also*, to indicate "Flying Butterfly," perform the double movement twice

Spider

Cross wrists, wriggle fingers in "walking" motion away from body

Plant

Right hand starts in flattened "O" below left hand "C," both palms in; right hand moves up and through left hand

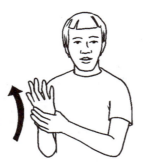

Flower

With the right thumb and finger-tips in flattened "O," touch face to right of, below, and left of nose

Tree

With right arm parallel to ground and right fingers to left elbow, hold left arm straight up and twist open "5" hand palm in and out several times

Grass

Heel of claw "5" right hand brushes up and across underside of chin to right, twice

2. Abstractions

The Signs for:
- *Feeling*
- *Thought*
- *Religion, Morality, and Philosophy*

Special Issue

Handshape and Location

The first two sections here pertain to feeling and thinking. The first sign that appears is for feeling. Flip forward and compare this one to the sign for thought (p.114).

The most obvious difference between them is their position relative to the body. This is a typical difference: signs describing mental activities are very often formed at or near the head (the "male" position in Sign) and the ones related to feelings are usually formed near the heart (the "female" position). This touch of gender bias is not unique to Sign. There is, in fact, a specific handshape called the *sensing* handshape, which is pictured among the handshapes in Chapter II. This handshape appears often on the next few pages. For signs that relate to mental activities, the pointing or index finger is frequently used.

Abstractions

Feeling

Feeling
Move "sensing" hand in a small arc in front of chest, ending with middle finger touching chest, twice

Joy
Flat right hand up and out at chest — *also* "Happiness"

Pleasure
Circle open palm on chest; may also use two hands, circling in opposite directions at stomach and chest levels — *also* as verb: "Enjoy," "Like"

Like
The "5" right hand starts with palm touching mid-chest, then moves out and into "8" shape with palm up

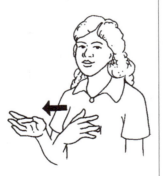

Want
Start "claw" hands palm up, out from body, pull straight in

Love
Cross hands at wrist, left over right, at heart level

Adore
Clasp right hand over left and move hands toward body in circular motion

Cherish

Both "claw" hands start palm in, right hand on chin, left at upper chest; both hands move down slightly, closing to "S" shape (may use just one hand)

I Love You

Palm out; thumb, little and index fingers up; middle fingers bent — *Note:* this basic handshape combines elements of the manual letters I, L, and Y held in the fingerspelling position

Proud, Pride

Thumb of extended "A" hand starts at lower torso and moves to upper chest

Hope

Start both "B" hands with fingers up, palms facing together; bend fingers down twice

Curious

Pinch neck with "F" hand thumb and index finger and wiggle slightly back and forth — *Note:* also means "I'm curious" / "Tell me" / "I'd like to know"

Eager

Rub palms together briskly with both hands straight and flat — *also* "Motivated"

Interest

Both "5" hands with bent middle fingers; start right hand at top, left at lower torso; pull both hands out from chest and into "8" shapes

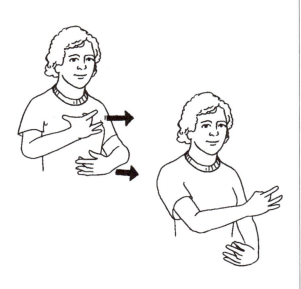

Anticipation

Right hand at mid-face, left higher; start all fingers straight up, then bend fingers forward twice — *also* "Expect," "Hope"

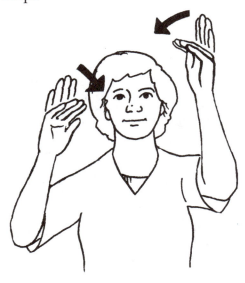

Surprise

Start hands closed, thumbs and index fingers pinched, near eyes; flick index fingers up

Thrilled

Both "sensing" handshapes, touch midchest and move up

Excited

Open hands, middle fingers bent; rotate in alternate circles, each striking chest repeatedly

Satisfied

Closed "B" hands start palms down, slightly apart, right hand above left; both move in toward chest

Respect

Start "R" hand up, curve outward from body, then down

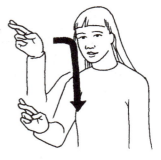

Discouraged

Both "5" hands; bend middle fingers, touch mid-chest and move downward — *also* "Depressed"

Disappointed

Palm toward body, touch index finger to chin — *also* "Miss"

Shame

Bent, closed "5" hands start palms in, back of fingers on cheeks; hands pivot down slightly until palms face out — *Note:* do with one hand to show less intense shame

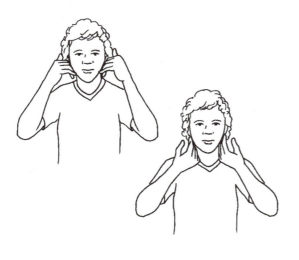

Disgusted

Right "claw" hand starts pressed to right upper chest; circle repeatedly

Fear

Both "5" hands palms out; move down in wavy motion

Despise

Open "5" hands start with palms facing, right higher than left and right thumb pulls away from under base of chin, then move down and away violently — *also* "Hate"

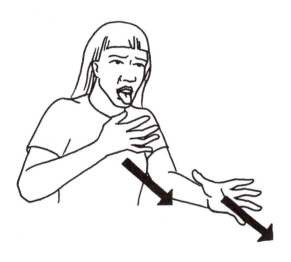

Sorrow

Start open "5" hands near face; bring down front of body, and show sadness on face — *also* "Sad"

Anger

Start "claw" hands at lower chest; bring up and out toward shoulders

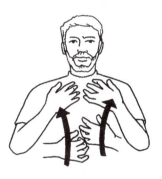

Hate

Both "8" hands, start with index fingers up then flick out to "5" shape, toward object of hate

Jealous

Start little finger at corner of mouth, palm left; pivot hand until palm is inward — *Note:* may also use bent "1" or "X" hand and same movement

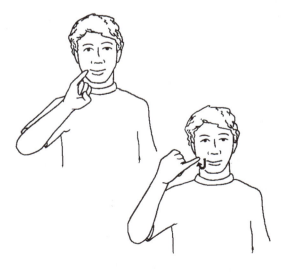

Troubled

Circle both "B" hands, alternating them in and out from forehead level down; keep palms facing each other

Frustrated
Back of open hand moves from below up, blocking mouth; may also use both hands alternately

Problem
Twist knuckles of bent double "X" fingers against each other in opposite directions

Thought

Thought
Index finger draws small circle at right forehead — *also* "Think"

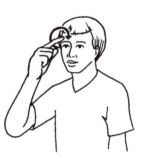

Mind
Right index finger to right temple, palm toward face, tap two times

Idea
Start "I" hand, little finger to forehead, then move up and out

Reason
Fingers of right "R" hand draw small circle at right forehead

Agree
Right "1" hand starts with index finger at right forehead; comes down to line up with left index finger, both pointing straight out

Decide

Right index finger touches forehead ("think") and moves down into "F" shape; then both "F" hands, palms facing together, move down firmly

Study

Wriggle fingers of right "5" hand (palm down) above palm of left "5" hand

Learn

Start fingers of right "claw" hand in palm of left closed "5" hand; bring right hand up into flattened "O" to touch right forehead

Read

Right hand "V" moves down, but not touching, the open left palm

Skillful

Right flat fingers close on little finger side of left hand, then pull away and down, closing into "A" — *also* "Skill"

Remember

Right thumb of "A" hand starts pressed to right forehead, moves down to thumb of left "A" hand and taps it twice

Forget

Right hand closed "5" starts flat on forehead; moves to right and closes to "A" shape

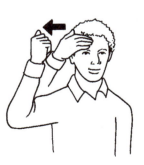

Memorize

Right "C" fingertips start at forehead; move out, closing to "S"

Know

Tap fingertips of bent "B" hand to forehead and nod — *Note:* to sign "Don't know," shake head side to side instead of nodding

Name

Noun: both "H" hands, palms facing together; tap right fingers on top of left two times — *also*, as verb, but tap once, then arc right hand outward once

Attention

Slide closed "5" hands straight out from temples twice

Language

Both "L" hands start thumbs together, wiggle outward

Information

Start both "O" hands in front of temples; move down and out, end with open palms up

Experience

Right hand open "5" fingers brush temple and cheek, pull slightly away to close to a flattened "O"

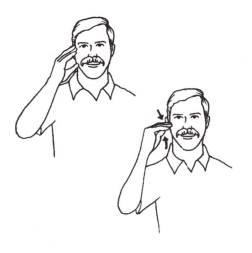

Understand

Start "S" hand near right forehead; flip finger up and nod head repeatedly — *Note:* to sign "Don't understand," shake head side to side instead of nodding

Suspect

Right "1" hand starts at right temple, pulls away and into "X" shape — also "Suspicion" if done twice

Expect

Right hand starts palm out, index finger up near brow, moves up above head changing to bent "B"; left hand bent "B" moves up slightly

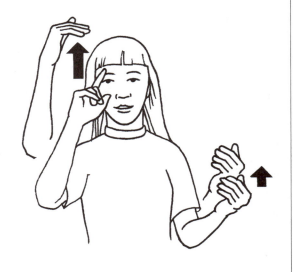

Imagination

Both "I" hands, right little fingers move from forehead up and out, alternately, twice

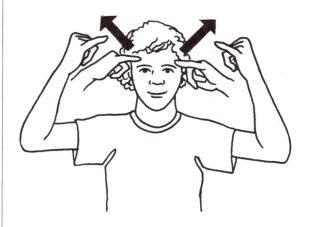

Dream

Pull extended index finger out from forehead, changing from "1" shape to "X" repeatedly as it goes out — *Note:* to sign "Nightmare," sign "Bad" plus "Dream"

Fantasy

Right hand "F" palm out at temple, then move out in small, spiraling movement

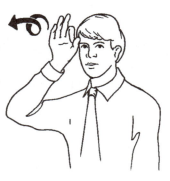

Wish

Right "claw" hand, palm in; move down to waist — *also* "Lust," when signed with both hands alternately

Religion, Morality, and Philosophy

Religion

Fingertips of "R" hand start at left chest over heart, palm in; move smoothly down and out until palm is down, fingers out

God

With palm left, arc the open right hand from over-head downward and toward face

Pray

Press palms together in prayer posture, then move in small circles, together repeatedly

Satan

Both "3" hands, thumbs at temples, close into claw "3" shapes — *Note:* may use just one hand

Sin

Both "X" hands start palms facing together, move together in small arcing motion

Holy

Right hand "H" starts palm in, fingers point left; left hand palm up, fingers out; right arcs out, down, brushing past left palm — *also* "Sacred," with "S" hand

Bible

Touch bent middle finger of "5" hand to palm, and then reverse ("Jesus" or "Stigmata"); then press palms together and open with little fingers touching, twice ("Book")

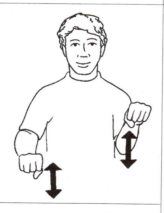

Faith

Start extended index finger to brow; change to "F" and move down to touch left "F" hand, twice — *Note:* as verb ("Have faith in"), use single movement

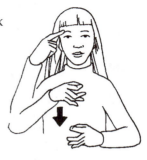

Believe

Touch extended index finger to brow ("Think"), bring down into clasp with left hand ("Marriage")

Doubt

Both "A" hands move up and down in alternating movements, palms down

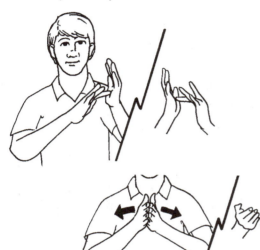

Peace

Start right and left palms pressed together, right facing out; pivot until left palm faces out, then both hands move down and apart; palms down

Soul

Right hand "F" pinches into left "C" hand, then moves out and up in wavy motion — *also* "Spirit"

Power

With left hand in "S" shape, right hand claw "C" starts palm down at upper chest; bends down toward left bicep

Energy

Start right hand "E" palm out near arm pit; bring down on top of left forearm

Glory

Right "sensing" handshape, middle finger starts at left palm, then moves right and up in wavy line

Temptation

Right index finger begins at left elbow, pulls right along bottom of angled left forearm, changing into "X" handshape

Philosophy

Right hand "P" starts at right temple, wrist bends repeatedly forward and down

Honest

Fingers of right "H" hand, palm left, move across upturned left palm from heel to fingers — *also* "Honesty," "Truth"

Real

Extended right index finger starts at lips and arcs up and out slightly — *also* "True," "Really"

Fair

Both hands bent; tap fingertips together repeatedly — *also* "Equal"

Right

Point both extended fingers out, strike right hand down on left — *also* "Correct"

Wrong

Tap middle fingers of "Y" hand to chin

Good

Start flat fingertips near lips, move down and out, stopping firmly with palm facing up

Bad

Start flat fingertips near lips, move down and out, turning palm down

Guilty

Tap right index finger on left upper chest several times

Innocent

Both "H" hands, palms in, at lips, left hand over right; hands move out, unbending at elbows, until palms are up, hands apart— *also* "Naive"

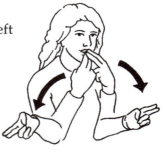

False

Start extended right index finger against side of cheek with palm slightly out and left; finger strikes cheek and nose and moves out

True

Index finger of right hand "D" starts near lips then makes a small arc out, up, and down — *also* "Real," "Really"

Purpose

Right hand "V" starts palm out with fingers to palm of left hand; right hand pivots on middle finger until right palm faces in

Promise

Start index finger to mouth, palm out; bring down while opening, and place on closed left hand

Responsibility

Fingertips of hands on right shoulder; tap hands or press slightly on shoulder indicating "weight" of responsibility — *also* "Liability"

Habit

Both "claw" hands palm down, right on top of left, move down to waist or lower

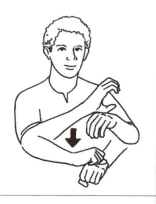

Choice

With right thumb and index finger (right palm down), touch left index and then middle finger (left palm in)

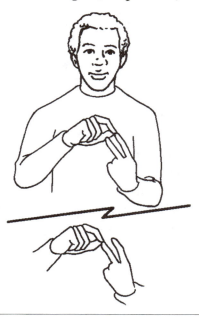

Judge

Both "F" hands, palms facing together, alternate moving up and down

Rules

Right hand "R," palm left, taps inside of fingertips then lower palm of left hand

Should

Tap "X" finger up and down twice — *also* "Need," "Must," "Ought to," "Gotta," "Have to"

Won't

Right hand "A," with palm left and thumb extended, strokes backward along jawline, but not touching

Law

Touch right hand "L" to fingers then heel of left open palm

Err

Right hand "Y" starts bent back against jawline, palm out slightly; pivots on chin until palm almost faces opposite direction — *also* "Wrong," "Oops"

Punishment

Right index finger takes a sweeping strike at left elbow

Terrible

Both hands start in "8" shape near temples, palms out; flick hands out and away from temples into open "5" shape — *also* "Awful," "Horrible"

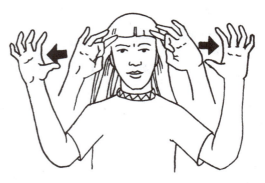

Wonderful

Both "5" hands, palms out; move out twice

Perfect

Both "P" hands, palms facing together; right index finger half-circles then touches left index finger

3. Action Verbs

The Signs for:
- *Moving and Doing*
- *Control, Compliance, and Competition*
- *Listing and Ordering, Beginning and Ending*
- *Communicating and Sensing*
- *Being, Having, Sharing, and Connecting*

Special Issue

Modified and Directional Verb Signs

First, a reminder about modified signs. Modified signs are the ones where a signer is called on to deliberately change the formation of a sign to make the meaning specific. The verbs *close* and *climb* were used as examples earlier; *open* and *wash* are other verbs we cite as modified in our dictionary. Exactly how you form these signs will depend on what you are closing or opening (a door or a window?), climbing (a ladder or a mountain?), or washing (your face or your car?). There are many, many modified signs.

Similarly, many verb signs are directional. When signing a directional verb, the onus is on the signer to form the sign in a way that is properly tailored to show who is performing the action or who is having it performed upon them (the subject and object). The signer generally does this by changing the palm orientation and the direction of the movement.

Deceive (p.135) and *show* (p.152) are the kinds of verbs (often ones that reflect physical actions) that are adapted to reflect the relationship between subject and object. The direction of the verb should leave no doubt, for instance, about who is deceiving whom, or who is showing what to whom.

Note also the signs for *give* and its variations (p.157) and *copy* and its variations (p.152-3), additional examples of how to change a sign directionally. Think of your goal this way: If you want to communicate that you gave your mother a gift, the movement must go *away* from you; if she gave it to you, you should make the movement *toward* yourself. Otherwise, your sign will simply be grammatically incorrect. But even if you don't study ASL grammar, the logic of this grammatical concept is apparent. If you are signifying something going in a particular direction, why move your hands in some other way? Your sign must match the particulars of what you mean. Remember, too, when forming modified and directional signs, maintain the integrity of your handshape.

One of the challenges for you as a new signer will be to remember to modify and direct your signs appropriately and in ways that accurately reflect your meaning. Good signers incorporate this concept into how they think and eventually do it automatically, without thinking.

Action Verbs

Moving and Doing

Do
Both "C" hands rock back and forth at lower chest — *Note:* hands may also move in small circles in same position

Can
Both "S" hands with palms facing down, move down together strongly

Create
Back of "4" hand moves from right temple up and out in arc

Discover
Loose, down-turned "5" hand moves up and back, changing into "F" shape

Build
Both "B" hands start at lower chest, right clasped over left; left moves on top of right, and right over left again as hands rise up to shoulder height

Prepare
Open hands, palms facing, fingers forward, move right in small arcs

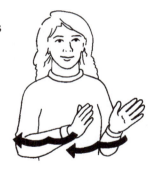

Cause

Both right "A" hands start palms up at mid-chest, then move out, opening into "5" shapes

Result

Start right "R" hand near left upper arm; pull straight across and straight down

Move

Both flattened "O" hands move forward in a wavy line — *also* "Put"

Go ahead, Get along

Both hands open, bent "B" with palms facing body, move forward smoothly

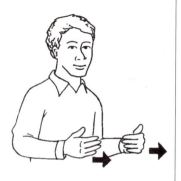

Come

Both extended index fingers start pointing out, palms up; then arc toward body with index fingers pointing down in front of body

Go

Both extended index fingers start pointing up, then arc down and out

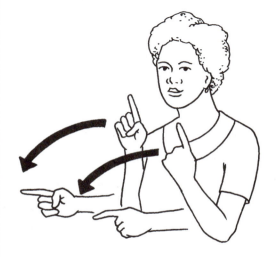

Left

"C" starts with palm facing right cheek, move out as fingers close to flattened "O" — *also* "Departed," "Went," "Gone," "Gone out"

Arrive

Bring right open hand, palm down, from midtorso down and rotate to end palm up in left palm

Visit

Move "V" hands outward, palms facing body, outward in alternating circles

Wait

Both "5" hands palm up; left forward of right and higher (shoulder height); wriggle fingers while moving hands in small circles

Leave

Both "5" hands, palms facing, move from body out — *also* "Abandon," "Neglect"

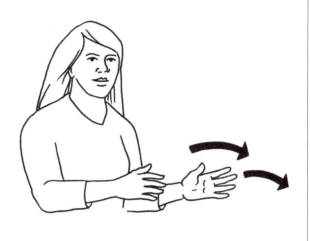

Follow

Both "A" hands, left in front of right, palms facing, move forward simultaneously; knuckles of right hand follow left wrist closely

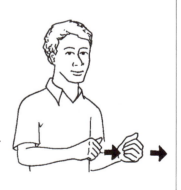

Stay

Both "Y" hands start palms down, thumbs touching, then right hand arcs out and down; may use one hand

Stop

Move little finger side of open right hand down firmly into palm-up, left hand — *also* "Halt," "Finish"

Sit

Right "H" hand taps on top of left "H" hand — *also* "Chair," but with two taps

Stand

Right "V" fingers, palm to body, touch (as if standing on) the up-turned palm of left hand

Dance

Right hand "V," palm in, swings slightly back and forth above palm of left hand "B"

Stop

Right hand "5" starts palm up, rotates strongly left until palm is slightly out and down — *also* "Desist," "Enough," "Quit"

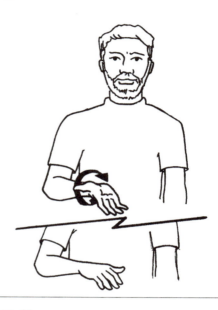

Walk

Alternately swing hands down, bending at wrists (as in the scuttle of feet)

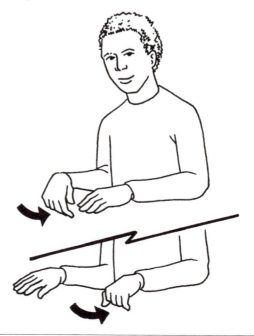

Run

Both "L" hands, hook right index on left thumb; move both hands forward repeatedly, crooking index fingers into "X" shapes

Play

Both "Y" hands; rotate wrists, hands moving from palm up to palm down

Jump

Right "V" fingers point down into left palm, pull up into bent double "X"; hop straight up and down

Jump off

Right "V" fingers point down into left palm, hop straight up and down, move off and outward in arc

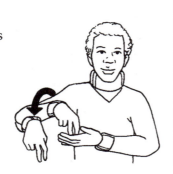

Fall (down)

Right hand "V" starts palm in, pressed to palm of left closed "5" hand, slides off end of left fingers, like person falling

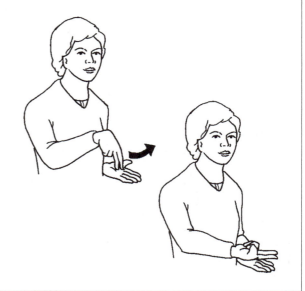

Fall (into)

Right hand bent double "X" starts palm up at upper chest, moves straight down through left hand "C"

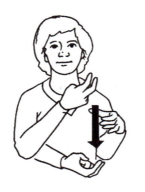

Climb

Both curved "5" hands alternate moving up in small arcs — *Note:* this sign is modified according to the exact thing being climbed

Race

Both "A" hands alternate moving quickly in and out, palms facing

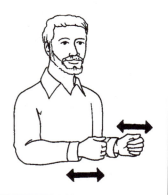

Pass (by)

Both "A" hands start palms facing, move forward

Drive

Fists parallel, palms facing each other; move straight out

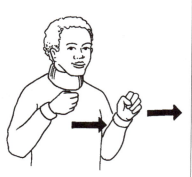

Park (a car)

Tap right hand "3," palm left and fingers forward, on upturned left palm

Fly (a plane)

With middle fingers bent, others extended, move hand from eye level out in extended

Fish

Start "T/X" hands raised, then arc them down with right hand "winding the reel"

Swim

Start both flat hands palms down; move back and forth (in and away) at waist height

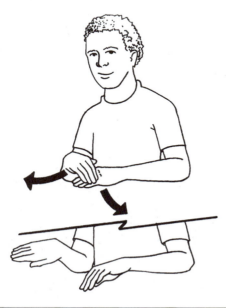

Hunt

Both "H" hands with thumbs up; move up and down (like shooting) repeatedly

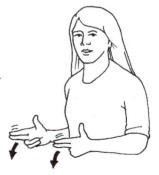

Camp

Extend index and little fingers, pull out and apart, once — *Note:* to mean "Camp" or "Tent," do twice

Train

Rub right "A" hand back and forth above index finger of left "B" hand — *also* "Practice," "Exercise"

Shower

Start right hand "S"; open into "5" over head on right, repeatedly

Rest

Fold arms at chest, palms inward

Wash

Palm-down right "A" hand circles counterclockwise above left "A" hand — *Note:* modify this sign according to the thing being washed

Sleep

Start claw "C" hand in front of face, bring down to just below chin, closing fingers to flattened "O"

Control, Compliance, and Competition

Control

Both "X" hands pointing forward, palms facing; move in and out in alternating movements

Force

"C" hand, palm forward, rolls over back of left, down turned hand until right hand is palm down

Change

Both "T/X" hands, keeping palms facing, rotate at wrist to reverse positions in relation to body

Tempt

Right "X" index finger taps left elbow twice

Annoy

Left hand palm toward body; right hand chops repeatedly between thumb and index of left hand — *also* "Bother," "Irritate"

Deceive

Start right hand "A" out from body, palm in and left "1" hand palm right; move right hand in to conceal left hand — *Note:* this is a directional verb, here meaning "To be deceived"

Deceive

Start right hand "A" near body, palm out and left "1" hand palm right, out from body; move right hand in to conceal left — *Note:* this is a directional verb, here meaning "To deceive"

Blame

Start right "A" hand little finger side on top of left "S" hand and move over and beyond left hand — *Note:* left hand may also be closed "5"

Sue

Left hand closed "5" palm right; right hand bent "B" strikes left palm

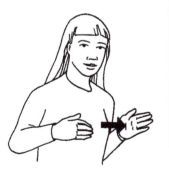

Defeat

Roll closed right hand across and down over downturned left hand

Kill

Slide right extended finger forward underneath fingers of flat, downturned left hand

Destroy

Right "claw" hand starts above left "claw" hand; right moves left, closing to "A"; comes back to left hand, now also "A," touching knuckles and moves out past left hand

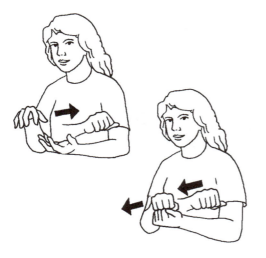

Break

Both "S" hands, thumbs together, palms down; move briskly out and down until palms face (as if breaking a stick)

Fix

Press fingertips of "O" hands together; move up and down alternately, fingertips striking in passing

Defend

Both "S" hands crossed at wrists at upper chest, right nearer body; move out slightly and stop firmly

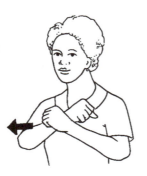

Endure

Right hand "A" thumbnail moves from lips down to chin

Depend

Outstretched right index finger on top of left; move hands and forearms down

Require

Left hand closed "5," palm right; thrust index finger of right "X" shape into left palm, pull right hand back "X" — *also* "Demand"

Help

Raise left hand "B" (palm up) to cradle right "A" hand — *also* "Assist"

Prevent

Hands start crossed, palms down, close to body at waist; move up and out, staying crossed

Save

Start closed hands crossed at chest; open wide, palms out — *also* "Free," "Freedom," but use "F" handshape, "Deliver" with "D" handshape

Succeed

Start both index fingers apart, pointing at each other at shoulder height; rotate hands at wrists until palms are out, fingers up

Improve

Start little finger side of open "B" right hand above and at right angle to back of left hand; right moves up left forearm in little jumps

Attempt

Start both "A" hands, palms facing; push forward in slight upward arc — *also* "Try" but with "T" handshape

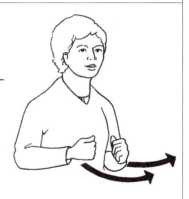

Win

Start right hand "5" up, palm left; sweep down, closing on top of closed left hand and back up and left

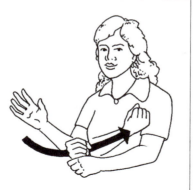

Celebrate

Both "T/X" hands make small circles at shoulder height — *also* "Festival," "Victory," "Anniversary"

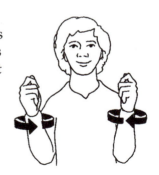

Fail

Right hand "V" palm up; stroke forward from heel to fingertips on palm of left hand

Graduate

Right hand "G" circles clockwise once above flat left palm, then drops down in left palm

Lose

Right hand "V" taps middle of palm of left closed "5" hand — *also* "Be defeated"

Flunk

Right hand "F" moves across front of body and forcefully against open left palm

Listing and Ordering, Beginning and Ending

List

Right bent "B" hand (palm in); start little finger on left fingertips and move down left palm to heel in little hops

Write

Right hand "T/X" shape starts at heel of left hand and squiggles down fingers and out — *Note:* add person marker to sign "Writer"

Count

Right hand "F" moves across left palm from heel to fingertips, repeatedly

Measure

Start "Y" hands, thumbs together, palms down; tap together twice

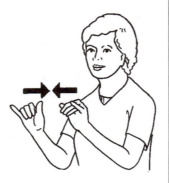

Compare

Start both bent "B" hands, palms facing together, right hand with palm out and left hand palm in; rotate hands to switch positions

Decrease

Both closed "5" hands, palms facing, right over left; right comes down to meet left — *also* "Reduce"

Increase

Start right hand "H" palm left, arc palm down to rest on left hand "H," hands rise slightly together — *also* "Add on," but without moving up; "Decrease," but with reversed movement

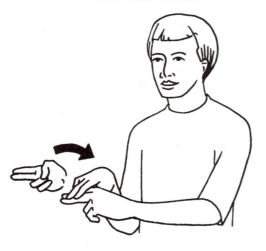

Add

Open right "5" hand starts palm down, moves up, closing to flattened "O," fingertips touching — *also* "Addition"

Subtract

Open "claw" right hand brushes past left "B" hand with palm facing right — *Note:* right hand may also be "A" or "S" shape

Repeat

Left hand "B," palm angled up and left; right hand bent "B," palm left, moves over and with fingertips strikes left palm — *also* "Again"

Schedule

Open right hand faces out; left hand faces in; right fingers slide down left palm, turn palm inward and pull sideways, describing a graph — *Note:* same for noun and verb

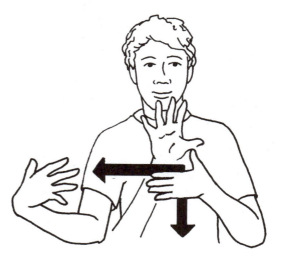

Pay

Extended right index finger starts on heel of palm-up left hand, sweeps forward across fingers and points out, palm down

Earn

Right hand claw "5," thumb up, sweeps from fingers around to heel, back to fingers of left palm and closes to "S"

Sell

Both flattened "O" hands start at shoulder height, palms facing body; rotate up until they are palms down

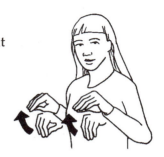

Buy

Right hand flattened "O," palm up, moves down and out along left palm

Splurge

Both "A" hands start tipped down slightly, palms facing, then rise up and out, ending in "5" shapes with palms facing

Begin

Index finger of right, palm-down hand rests between left middle and index fingers, then right hand twists so palm ends up — *also* "Start," "Initiate"

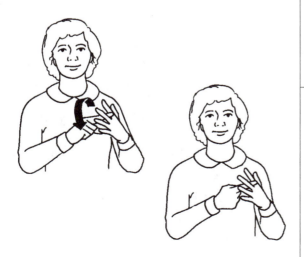

Save (money)

Push right flattened "O" hand into left "C" hand twice — *also* "Invest"

Continue

Both "A" hands, palms down, thumbs together, move out smoothly from body

Happen
Both "1" hands, index fingers point out, palms facing; pivot inward simultaneously until both palms are down — *also* "Occur," "Event"

Evolve
Both "E" hands, palms facing, right above left, then rotate left on top — *Note:* to sign "Reverse," use "R" hand; "Modify," "M"; or "Change," "T/X"

Become
Closed "5" hands start at throat level, palms together; wrists rotate until palms face opposite directions

End
Both "B" hands crossed, right resting at angle on top of left; slide right along top of left, then down past end of left fingers — *also* "Complete," "Finish"

Close

Flat, palm-down closed "B" hands come together briskly — *Note:* this sign is modified according to the exact thing being closed — *also* "Shut"

Open

"B" hands, palms down and thumbs together; arc out and open until palms face each other — *Note:* modify to fit the circumstances (*see* "Close")

Quit

Start fingers of right hand "H" (palm left) clasped in left hand "C"; pull out and arc up and back slightly

Postpone

Both "F" hands, palms facing, move from near body outward — *also* "Procrastinate"

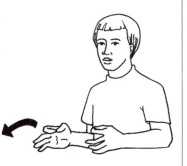

Cancel

Extended right index finger draws large "X" on left palm

Communicating and Sensing

Communicate

Both "C" hands, palms facing, alternate moving from just in front of corner of mouth, out, and back

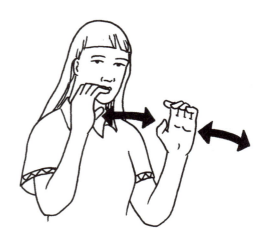

Sign

With index fingers up, alternate circling hands toward body

Lip read, Speech read

With bent double "X" fingers, make small clockwise circle around mouth

Hear

Right hand "C" cupping right ear

Talk

Right hand "4" starts palm facing left near middle of mouth and moves straight out, twice

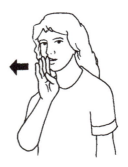

Inform

Start fingers of flattened "O" right hand at forehead and flattened "O" left hand palm up at midchest; move both down and out and into "5" shapes — *also* "Tell," "Information"

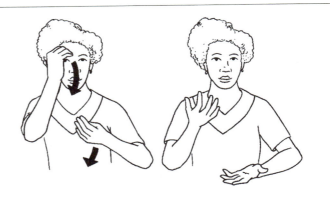

Announce

Start both "1" hands with index fingers at mouth, arc out

Interpret

Both "F" hands; start right hand palm out, left in; pivot hands to switch positions relative to body, repeatedly — *also* "Interpreter" when person marker is added

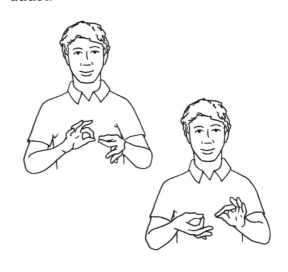

Quote

Crook first two fingers of both hands twice to indicate quote marks

Explain

Hold both "F" hands with palms facing; move back and forth, alternating — *also* "Describe"

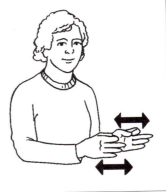

Describe

Both "F" hands, palms facing, move alternating in and out from body — *also* "Explain"

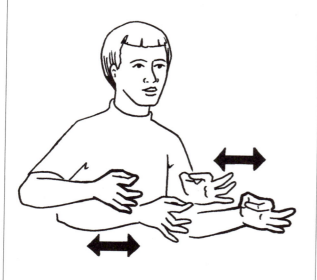

Guess

Right hand "C" moves from right of face in arc, left and down, closing into "S"

Ask

Start "1" finger pointing up and out, then crook finger slightly and draw a question mark

Answer

Palms of hands facing out, start right index finger at mouth, left lower and forward; move down in arcs — *also* "Tell"

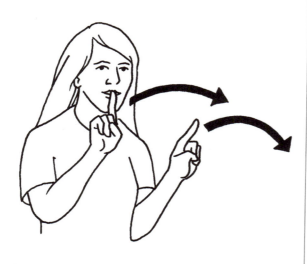

Gossip

Both "G" hands, pinch fingers open and closed repeatedly while circling hands — *also* "Rumor"

Lie

Draw index finger of "D" hand from right to left in front of mouth (can also use bent "B")

Argue

Index fingers point toward each other and move, alternating up and down

Order

Bring extended index finger from lips down and forward

Interrupt

Both "B" hands, left angled down slightly; right chops once or twice against thumb side of left

Mock

Both "ILY" hands with thumbs folded; palms down, right slightly higher than left; both hands move from body away, twice

Complain

Tap fingertips of "claw" hand repeatedly against chest; use both hands alternately for greater intensity of complaint — *also* "Whine"

Warn

Tap right index finger repeatedly against left hand, which has palm right and fingers up — *also* "Signal," "Alarm"

Insult

Right hand "1" starts palm down, index finger out, then curves out and up sharply

Scream

Start "claw" hands near chin, move up and out; may also use only one (the dominant) hand

Deny

Thumbs of both "A" hands start under chin, move out and off to their respective sides

Admit

Both bent "B" hands start with palms facing body, then move out and down until palms are up and fingers pointing out — *also* "Confess"

Apologize

Right hand "S" at heart level circles repeatedly — *also* "Sorry"

Cry

Both hands move up and down cheeks alternately, taking "X" shape when down, "1" when up

Laugh

Both bent "B" hands start with palms facing body at corners of mouth; pull straight out and rotate wrists back, repeatedly

Smile

Bent "B" hands start with fingertips at mouth corners, then pull up as if stretching mouth into a smile (*do* smile!)

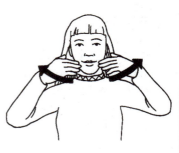

Sing

Right open hand swings, palm toward body, up and down left forearm — *also* "Song," "Music" (right hand "M"); and "Poetry" (with "P")

Praise

Pat palms together repeatedly — *also* "Applaud," "Hearing Applause," "Commend"

See

Start "V" fingers at face level, middle finger touches cheek below eye, moves in arc outward

Notice

Lower index finger of right hand "X" from right eye to palm of left hand — *also* "Recognize"

Watch

Both "V" hands, start right hand just below right eye, left just below chin, move both out, twice

Cook

Press palm of right "B" hand to palm of left, then flip on its back and back to palm, twice; left hand remains stationary

Smell

With fingers pointing left, raise right palm up slightly in front of nose twice

Taste
Bend middle finger of "sensing" hand to lower lip

Eat
Place right hand flattened "O" at lips

Imbibe, Drink alcohol
Right hand "Y," palm left, thumb at corner of mouth, tip back in "tippling" motion, with eyes closed

Kiss
Fingertips of flattened right "O" hand touches **lips then left, flattened "O" fingertips**

Touch
Bring extended middle finger down to back of left hand

Pet
Flat open right hand drags on back of left hand "S," inward

Being, Having, Sharing, and Connecting

Be, Am, Are
Right index finger, palm right, starts at lips and moves straight out

Seem
Hold right hand slightly bent fingers up with palm out; pivot until palm faces inward — *also* "Appear"

Appear
Closed "5" hands begin right palm out and left palm in, pivot at wrists to switch palm orientation — *also* "Appearance"

Disappear
Start extended right index finger between left index and middle fingers; pull down while crooking into "X" shape — *also* "Vanish"

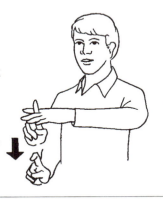

Prove
Right hand "B" starts up high with palm in, fingers up, moves down into left palm

Hide
Thumb of right "A" hand starts at lips, moves out and down into clasp with left hand

Show

With extended right index finger touching left palm (palm out), arc both down and forward slightly; directional verb meaning, as pictured here, "I show you"

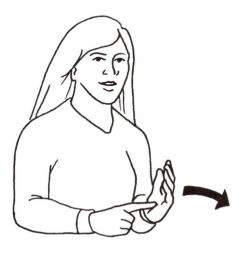

Show

With extended right index finger touching left palm (palm in), arc both up and in toward the body slightly; directional verb meaning, as pictured here, "You show me"

Copy

Right hand claw "5" starts fingertips pressed to inward-facing palm of left hand "B," then pulls back and into flattened "O"; directional verb meaning, as pictured here, "I copy you"

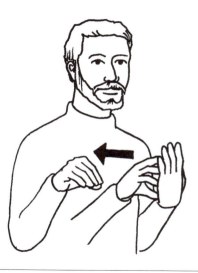

Copy

Right hand claw "5" starts fingertips pressed to outward-facing palm of left hand "B," then pulls out and into flattened "O"; directional verb meaning, as pictured here, "You copy me"

Photocopy

Right hand claw "5" starts fingertips pressed to downward-facing palm of left hand "B," then pulls down and into flattened "O"; this is another directional variation of "Copy"

Fax

Left hand "B"starts over back of right at right angle, hands move out in wavy line — *Note:* literally means "Paper coming out"; often fingerspelled

Accept

Start both closed "5" hands palms down at collarbone level, bring down and in toward chest, changing to flattened "O" shapes

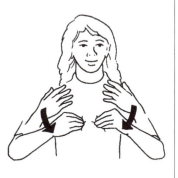

Reject

Point thumb of right "A" hand back over shoulder, keeping palm left

Rather

Bent "B" hand starts at center of chest, moves out closing into "A" shape with thumb extended — *also* "Prefer"

Prefer

Right "sensing" hand with middle finger just below mouth — *also* "Rather"

Vote

Right hand "F" moves down into opening of left hand "O" — *Note:* to sign as noun, do twice

Allow

Both hands open, parallel at sides, move out and up in small arc

Obey

Both closed "5" hands start out, palms down, right near forehead, move straight down, bowing head— *also* "Obedient"

Cooperate

Interlock "F" fingers of both hands and rotate hands counterclockwise in front of body

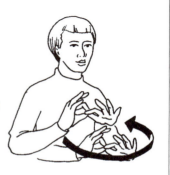

Introduce

Closed "5" hands start out with palms down, then swing in big arc down and forward, rotating hands so palms end facing up

Meet

Both "1" hands start out at shoulder width, move together (as people coming face to face)

Flirt

Both "5" hands, thumbs touching, palms horizontal; wiggle fingers

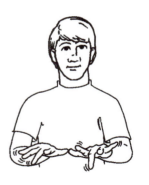

Marry

Bring slightly curved open hands together in firm clasp

Raise (a child)

Closed "5" hand starts palm down at waist; pulls straight up, angling back slightly — *also* "Rear"

Divorce

Start both "D" hands, palms facing, with index fingers pointing up; palms rotate out at wrist

Join

Right "H" fingers start pointing up, palm left, then move down into center of left hand "C" — *also* "Participate," when signed with right hand "P"

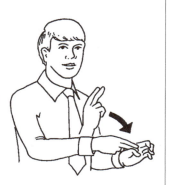

Attach

With right palm out and left in, "8" hands touch thumbs and index fingers together, then open and close, linking together

Separate

Bent "B" hands start with knuckles together, then pull apart to the sides, hands closing to "A" shapes

Has, Have

Curved closed "5" hands press fingers into open chest — *also* "Own," "Possess"

Take

Start right hand "5" open and out, palm down; pull in and close to "S" shape

Steal

Right hand "V" starts palm in, in front of left elbow, then pulls rightward along left forearm and upward, changing to bent "V"

Own

Right hand "A," palm in, left hand "1"; right hand moves down with back of right knuckles tapping left index finger — *also* "Possess," "Have"

Keep

Both "K" hands; little finger side of right hand and index finger side of left tap repeatedly

Lose

Touch knuckles of both "C" hands together, palms in; bring down and apart, fingers down — *also* "Misplace"

Use

Circle right hand "U," palm left, behind closed left hand

Offer

With both open palms up, arc forward and up

Get

Both "5" hands palms facing, right above left; bring hands toward chest, both closing into "S" shapes — *also* "Receive"

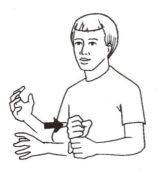

Send

Right hand bent "B" starts touching back of left hand near wrist; straighten wrist to point fingers out, twice

Give

Flattened "O" hand starts at chest; moves out, palm up (may use both hands with identical movements)

Deliver

Start "A" hands crossed at wrists, palms as pictured or both palms out; open arms and raise arms until both palms face out — *also* "Free" (verb)

Carry

Both hands palm up, move in arc from left to right

Share

Move flat right hand between left index finger and thumb several times, keeping hands perpendicular

Borrow

Cross "K" hands at wrist, bring toward body — *Note:* reverse movement (move hands away from body) to sign "Lend"

Exchange

Both "F" hands; right hand starts close in, left out more; then hands switch in-out locations

4. Describers

The Signs for:
- *Human Qualities and Sensations*
- *Numbers, Amount, Degree, and Relation*
- *Shape, Size, Condition, and Color*
- *Time, Tempo, and Pace*

Special Issues

The Order of Modifiers

In ASL, the placement of adjectives and adverbs in relation to the words they modify is quite different from the placement in English. In both English and Sign, for instance, modifiers are placed near the thing they modify. However, in English, adjectives *always* precede nouns; in Sign, an adjective is signed more often than not after a noun. For instance, in ASL you want to refer in sign to "the tall man" indicating a man standing in a crowd of people. Because you are using "tall" to distinguish one man from others, you would sign *tall* after *man* — saying, in a sense, "the man who is tall." However, whenever you sign a noun as an adjective, you should always sign it *before* the noun sign. For example, you would sign *vacation money* or *dinner music*.

Modifying the Modifiers

There are numerous ways to enhance the meanings of adjectives and adverbs. To intensify a quality, for example, you can add the sign *very*. However, it is more customary to modify the adjectival or adverbial sign itself to add to its meaning. For instance, the sign for *blue* involves pivoting the wrist back and forth; if you make this motion just slightly you will be indicating

bluish or *light blue*. Or, if you elongate the movement, you are describing a blue that is darker and more intense.

Facial expression, too, is a prime way to enhance the meaning of a modifier. For instance, you may sign *dirty* with your brow slightly furrowed; or, you can turn your mouth down and squint; with the latter facial expression, you will be communicating *filthy*.

Changing hand position is another way to indicate degree of meaning. For instance, the signs to show size (*small*, *large*, *huge*) are basically very similar. As your hands move further apart, the thing described becomes larger. Notice, too, how the signer's facial expressions differ.

Dates and Addresses

Forming numbers larger than 9 is explained in this section. When you use these numbers (teens, twenties, thirties, hundreds, thousands, and so on) in expressing dates and addresses, you often sign in a way patterned after commonly spoken English. For instance, to refer to the year 2012 you will first sign *twenty*, then *twelve*. If your address is 546 Dylan Thomas Street, you'll sign *five*, then *forty-six*, as opposed to signing *five, four, six*.

A Special Way to Modify Numbers

There is an elegant and efficient way to indicate amounts of some particular things in Sign: namely, you can incorporate the appropriate numeral handshape into a sign for the thing you are counting or measuring. For instance, if you sign *hour* using a "2" handshape, you will communicate *two hours*; sign *year* with a "4" shape, and you mean *four years*. This holds true also for months, days, minutes, and weeks (see p.175).

Describers

Human Qualities and Sensations

Polite
Thumb of right hand "5" taps center of chest and moves up slightly, twice

Cheerful
Both "5" hands, palms in at shoulder height; wriggle fingers and hands, moving up and back repeatedly — *also* "Friendly"

Kind
Both "B" hands start palms in; right "B" hand goes over and around left

Meek
Both "B" hands, left hand bent palm down, right hand palm left; right index finger starts at mouth then moves down beneath left hand — *also* "Humble"

Secret
Tap right hand "A" thumbnail twice against lips

Nervous
Both "5" hands start palms down (palms may also face together slightly); wrists make small, quick rotations so that hands tremble noticeably

Calm

Start both "B" hands crossed just below face, right hand closer in; both hands move down, and then down and out, palms opening

Vain

Start both "V" hands above shoulders, palms angled down; bounce up and down simultaneously, twice

Sarcastic

Both hands "ILY"; palm out, right hand moves from corner of mouth, arcs downturning palm up to rest on back of left, palm down hand

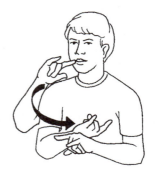

Selfish

Both "3" hands start palms down, out from waist; draw toward body, bending fingers

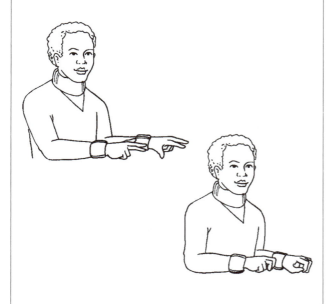

Stubborn

Press thumb of closed "5" hand to right temple; then bend fingers down — *also* "Donkey," "Male"

Boring

Index finger touches right side of nose, palm out; pivots palm in repeatedly

Funny

Move extended index and middle fingers down the nose, twice

Silly

Right hand "Y" arcs back and forth in front of face

Nude

Use wrist to move middle finger of right hand "5" across back of left hand "5" — *also* "Empty," "Bare"

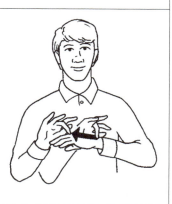

Smart

Start bent middle finger of open hand at forehead, flick palm open — *also* "Intelligent"

Stupid

Knock closed "A" hand gently against forehead

Confused

Both "claw" hands, right palm facing down and left palm up; hands circle so that right is away from body while left is near, and vice versa

Ignorant

Tap back of "V" hand to forehead

Qualified

Right hand clasps outer side of left, which is "B" shape facing right; right then pulls away — *also* "Ability," "Skill," "Skillful," "Qualification"

Tired

Bent curved "5" hands start with fingers pressed to chest, pivot out at wrists until backs of hands face each other and fingers point up

Careless

Both "V" hands, palms facing, move in and out from sides of head to below jawline, alternating positions

Lonely

"1" finger, palm left, moves from lips slowly and smoothly down in circular movement

Overwhelmed

Both hands "5," palms down, raise straight up

Insane

Right hand "4" starts palm down, fingers level with and pointing at eyes; arm pivots at elbow so hand goes back and forth in front of eyes

Poor

Right hand grasps left elbow with open fingers, then pulls down and away, closing fingers, twice

Broke (moneyless)

Fingers of bent "B" hands start over shoulder, tap neck

Rich

Right hand "A" starts in palm of closed "5" left hand, then arcs up and slightly right in "claw" shape

Deaf

"1" right hand, palm out, pointing up, moves from ear to mouth (mouth to ear also okay)

Blind

Start bent double "X" right hand out slightly from face and bring in close to eyes (as if "putting eyes out")

Famous

Start extended fingers at mouth corners, palms in, then move forward, out, and up in a big spiral

Oral

Flattened "O" hand starts beside corner of mouth and arcs in circular movement

Shy

Back of fingers press cheek, then head and shoulder compress toward hand, back nearly to neck

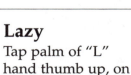

Embarrassed

Palms toward face, both open "5" hands move in alternating circles, always rolling up toward face and away

Eager

Rub palms together, hands flat, fingers pointing — *also* "Motivated," "Enthusiasm," "Enthusiastic"

Strict

Start bent double "X" hand fingers up, palm left; bring down onto bridge of nose

Weak

Fingers of right hand, palm in, touch left palm, then crumple forward — *also* "Feebleminded," when placed on forehead

Lazy

Tap palm of "L" hand thumb up, on shoulder twice

Strong

Start both claw "C" hands with finger-tips on shoulders, move both hands up and out with force from shoulders, changing them to "S" shapes

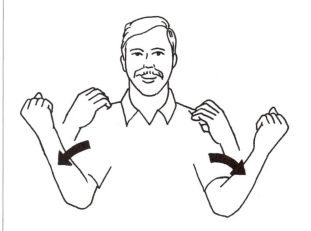

Idle

Palms open, fingers up, press thumbs near armpits, tap inward twice while wiggling fingers — *also* "Leisure time," "Vacation"

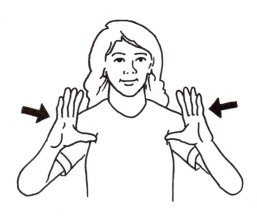

Busy

Both "B" hands, right palm out, left palm down; with heel near thumb side of left hand, right hand moves back and forth

Hungry

With palm in, move "C" hand from upper chest straight down to lower chest

Thirsty

Move extended index finger from under chin on throat to base of throat

Mature

Index finger of right "M" hand, palm down, moves from heel to finger-tips of out-facing left palm

Old

Right hand "C" moves down from chin in a slightly wavy motion to midtorso

Young

Both hands open, bent; brush fingertips up shoulders, twice — *also* "Youthful," "Teenaged" (but with "T" handshapes)

Pregnant

Closed "5" hand starts near waist and arcs out, describing shape of belly

Beautiful

Right hand "5" starts up, slightly to right of face; circles in front of face, coming down to flattened "O" shape slightly left of chin

Cute

"U" hand starts at chin, palm in; moves down closing into "A"; may repeat for emphasis

Ugly

Start with index finger pointing left in front of face; pull hand right, curling index finger into "X"

Cool

With open flat hands, fan the face, bend at wrist

Comfortable

Curved closed right hand slides palm down across back of left fingers; left hands does same to right — *also* "Comfort"

Wet

Both claw "5" hands palm up move down as fingers close to flattened "O," twice

Hot

Right hand claw "5" starts palm facing in, thumb below lips; moves right, down, and out, ending palm down

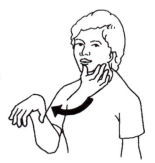

Dry

Draw extended right index finger across chin, from left to right, closing into "X" shape

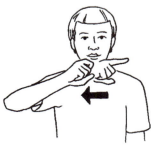

Dirty

Open "5" hand with back of hand under chin, palm down, wiggle fingers alternately

Clean

Palm of right open hand slides from heel across fingers of left palm, twice — *also* "Nice," but make movement only once

Sharp

Middle finger of right "sensing" hand starts pressed to back of left hand; arcs outward (as if reacting to sharpness)

Rough

Right "claw" hand starts at heel of palm-right "B" left hand; right hand moves out along line of left fingers

Smooth

Both closed "5" hands; right circles back of left

Soft

Both hands palm up in open "5/C" shapes; hands move down slightly, closing into flattened "O" shapes

Hard

Strike middle finger of right "V" hand against side of left bent "V" hand

Heavy

Both closed "5" hands, palms up; start with shoulders hunched up, lower shoulders as if being pressed down; hands shift down only slightly

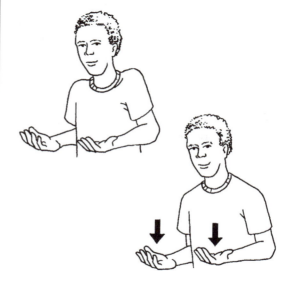

Light

Both "sensing" hands, palms angled down and facing; rotate hands to palms up, raising arms slightly

Sour

Index finger at chin rotates back and forth beneath pursed lips — *also* "Bitter"

Noisy

Start right "1" hand pointing at right ear; move both "5" hands out and down, shaking them

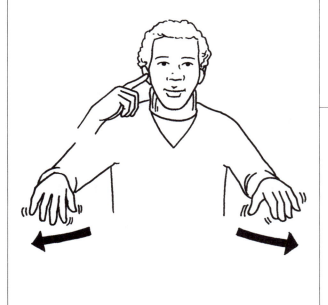

Quiet

Start "B" hands crossed in front of mouth, then move out and down, palms down — *also* "Calm"

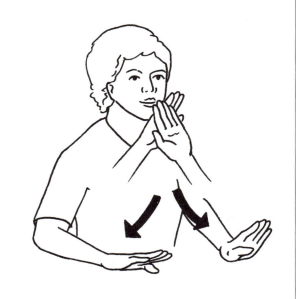

Numbers, Amount, Degree, and Relation

Ten
Right hand "A" with extended thumb up shakes back and forth slightly

Eleven
Flick index finger against thumb and up, twice

Twelve
Flick fingers of "2" hand against thumb and up, twice

Thirteen
Fingers (but not thumb) of the "3" hand flick down toward the palm and back up, twice

Fourteen
Fingers of the "4" hand flick down toward the palm, twice

Fifteen
Fingers of the "5" hand flick down toward the palm, twice

Sixteen

Right hand "10" starts palm left, then pivots until palm is out, changing into a "6" shape — *Note:* the variation of "Sixteen" is used as commonly

Sixteen

Right hand "6" starts palm left, then pivots until the palm is out

Seventeen

Right hand "10" starts palm left, then pivots until palm is out, changing into a "7" shape — *Note:* the variation of "Seventeen" is used as commonly

Seventeen

Right hand "7" starts palm left, then pivots until palm is out

Eighteen

Right hand "10" starts palm left, then pivots until palm is out, changing into an "8" shape — *Note:* the variation of "Eighteen" is used as commonly

Eighteen

Right hand "8" starts palm left, then pivots until palm is out

Nineteen

Right hand "10" starts palm left, then pivots until palm is out, changing into a "9" shape — *Note:* the variation of "Nineteen" is used as commonly

Nineteen

Right hand "9" starts palm left, then pivots until palm is out

Twenty
Right hand "G," palm left, thumb and index finger open and close repeatedly

Twenty-one
Palm-in "L" hand bends thumb down at first joint only, repeatedly

Twenty-two
Right hand "2" starts with the palm out, then pivots/bounces slightly to the right

Twenty-three
Right hand "3" palm out; middle finger bends down repeatedly

Twenty-four
Thumb of palm-out "L" hand closes into palm as three fingers that were down come up into the "4" shape

Twenty-five
Index and ring finger of "5" hand bend down toward the palm repeatedly

Twenty-six
Thumb of palm-out "L" hand closes onto little finger as three middle fingers rise into the "6" shape

Twenty-seven
Thumb of the palm-out "L" hand closes onto ring finger as three remaining fingers rise into the "7" shape

Twenty-eight

Thumb of palm-out "L" hand closes onto middle finger as three remaining fingers rise into the "8" shape

Twenty-nine

Thumb of the palm-out "L" hand and index finger close together as three remaining fingers rise into the "9" shape

Thirty

Right hand "3" closes into a flattened "O" shape

Thirty-three, forty-four, fifty-five, sixty-six, seventy-seven, eighty-eight, ninety-nine

To sign "thirty-three," the "3" hand starts with the palm facing out, then pivots/bounces slightly to the right, keeping the "3" shape (showing two threes); to sign "forty-four," the "4" completes the same motion; and so on

Thirty-one, etc.

To sign "thirty-one," start with a "3" hand and change it into a "1" shape; to sign "thirty-two," the hand changes from "3" into a "2"; (for "thirty-three" see the following entry); for "thirty-four," the hand changes from "3" into "4." This same pattern is used for the forties, the fifties, on up to the nineties, with a few irregular numbers, shown in the following pages.

"Irregular" numbers

There are two groups of numbers that are signed in an irregular fashion (that is, they don't follow any of the patterns already shown here). Group 1 includes the numbers 67, 68, 69, 78, 79, 89; Group 2 includes 76, 86, 87, 96, 97, 98. The next four entries will show examples from each group, from which signing the others in that group can be extrapolated.

Sixty-seven

"6" hand starts palm left, then arcs slightly left, ending palm out in the "7" shape — *Note:* applying this formula to the numbers 68, 69, 78, 79, 89; 68 is shown next

Sixty-eight

"6" hand starts palm left, then arcs slightly left, ending palm out in the "8" shape

Seventy-six

"7" hand starts palm out, then arcs slightly left, ending palm left in the "6" shape — *Note:* applying this formula to the numbers 86, 87, 96, 97, 98; 86 is shown next

Eighty-six

"8" hand starts palm out, then arcs slightly left, ending palm left in the "6" shape

One hundred

The "1" hand opens into a "C" shape

One thousand

Right hand bent "B" arcs onto palm of left hand closed "5," which is palm up

Two hours

Circle right hand "2" above left palm, ending with right palm to left *palm*— *Note:* this sign, and the two that follow ("six days," "four years") were created by modifying an existing sign (here "hours") with a new handshape (the shape of the desired number; on the dominant hand)

Six days

Start right hand "6" over left arm; lower right hand, pointing fingers left — *Note:* this is a number-modified version of "Days"

Four years

The right hand "4" starts out resting on left hand "S," then circles forward and under the left, returning to its original position — *Note:* this is a number-modified version of "Years"

Number

Both hands, with thumbs and fingers together, touching

Once

Strike index finger of "1" hand against left palm and bring back up

Twice
Start right "2" hand fingers up, palm in; bring down to strike upturned left palm, raise back up

None
Both "O" hands, palms at angle facing out, move out to the sides

Enough
Palm down, right hand pushes down across top of left hand "S," palm right — *also* "Sufficient"

Much
Start both "claw" hands with fingers touching; move out, apart, in arcs

More
Tap fingertips of flattened "O" hands together several times

Many
Start both "S" hands; open into claw "5" shapes and close, several times

Most
Both "A" hands; start right hand below left; arc right hand up past left hand, keeping thumb up

Each other
Circle right thumb over left, keeping left palm in, right palm out — *also* "Fellowship," "Interact"

Both

Start right hand "V" and closed "5" hands both palm in, right behind left; slide right hand down past and below left, bringing fingers together to "U" handshape

Each

Both "A" hands, palms facing; pivot right hand at wrist so that right thumb brushes down against left thumb — *also* "Every"

Different

Start extended index fingers crossed, move out and away from each other, keeping palms out

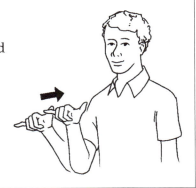

Alike

Both "1" hands start touching and pointing out; move both hands slightly left and tap together, then right and tap together — *also* "As"

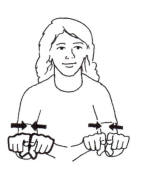

Same

Move "Y" hand back and forth, palm down — *also* "Like" as in "Looks like"

Exact

Right hand "T/X," palm out, circles then moves down toward left hand "T/X" — *also* "Precise"

Equal

Tap fingertips of bent "B" hands together just below chin height, keeping palms facing — *also* "Fair"

Few

Start "A" hand, palm up; quickly, smoothly roll fingers open, starting with index finger; move thumb over to palm — *also* "Several"

Every

Both "A" hands; left hand palm right, right hand palm in; right hand moves down to midchest

Any

Start "A" palm up with extended thumb; arc until palm is down and thumb left

Another, Other

Start extended thumb of "A" hand pointing left, roll up and over so thumb is pointing right

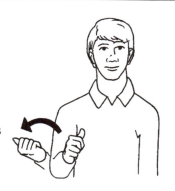

Whole

Right hand "5" sweeps straight across (right to left) top of left hand "O" — *also* "Entire"

Almost

Both hands open, slightly bent; right comes from below, brushes back of left hand and rises to just above fingertips of left hand

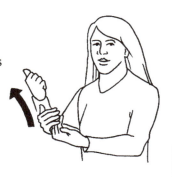

Very

Start both "V" hands with fingertips touching midchest; pull apart, up, and out

Also

Palms down, tap index fingers together in front of body, then to the right — *also* "Alike"

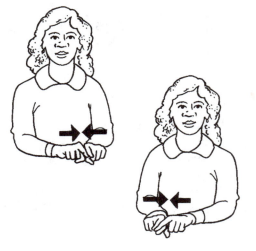

Empty

Move bent middle finger of right "sensing" hand down the back of left, closed "5" hand

Full

Right hand "B," palm down; left hand "S," palm right; right sweeps top of left hand from right to left

Except

With right hand "F," tug up on left index finger — *also*, "Special"

Limited

With right bent hand above left, palms facing, pivot both hands out slightly at wrists

Difficult

Bent "V" (or bent double "X") hands move up and down in front of body, knuckles striking each other in passing

Dangerous

Right hand "A" starts in front of left hand "A," with both palms down; right thumb brushes back of left hand toward body

Safe

Both "S" hands start crossed at chest; open out to sides — *also* "Save," "Rescue"

Important

Start both "F" hands, palms facing, curve up until palms face down and thumb sides of hands are together

Favorite

Touch middle bent finger of "5" hand to chin several times

Cheap

Right hand starts palm up, swings down brushing little fingers on left palm, ends palm down

Necessary

Move "X" index finger up and down twice — *also* "Need," "Must," "Should," "Ought to"

Easy

Brush palm of right hand upward along back of left fingers, twice

Familiar

Bent closed "5" right hand starts with fingers to right brow, moves out to right — *also* "Know"

Regular

Both index fingers extended, pointing out; tap twice right down on left as hands move forward slightly

Odd

Right hand "C" starts near right side of face, palm left, then arcs so palm is down in front of face — *also* "Strange"

Shape,
Size,
Condition,
and
Color

Shape

Move "A" hands, thumbs out, palms facing out from shoulders, down in wavy motion

Fat

Left hand palm up; right "Y" hand palm down, rock right hand back and forth from heel of left hand to fingertips — *also* "Obese"

Thin

Both "I" hands; start knuckles of right hand directly above knuckles of left; move right down, left up, until knuckles meet

Large

Thumb and forefinger of both "C" hands, palms facing, at sides — *Note:* notice the similarities between "Large," "Huge," and "Small"; this is a group of signs modified to accurately reflect the degree of size

Huge

Thumb and forefinger of both "C" hands, palms facing, held wide apart

Small

Both "5" hands, close together, palms parallel

Narrow

Both hands flat at sides, palms facing and thumbs up; move closer in together

Tall

Slide right hand "1" (palm left) up the palm (facing right) of the left hand

Short

Right hand palm down at right side, bounces down slightly — *also* "Small" (in stature)

Long

Right hand "L" moves from back of left hand "B" up past elbow

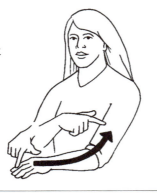

Deep

Right hand "1" starts pointing down, left at midchest, palm in; right sweeps down to below waist, left moves down slightly

Broad

Closed "5" hands start at midchest with palms together, fingertips touching; hands swing open until palms are out and thumbs stay up

New

With both hands palm up, right hand slightly right of and above the left hand, right hand arcs down into left palm and up

Black

Slide LEFT index finger right to left, across forehead

White

Closed "5" hand starts palm in at upper chest, pulls out and closes into a flattened "O"

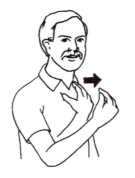

Gray

Both "5" hands, palms facing in; right starts near body, left away; right hand moves out as left moves in, passing through each other's fingers

Color
Right hand "5" open; wriggle fingers in front of chin

Green
With fingers pointing out, "G" hand rotates at wrist so that palm moves from facing left to facing out

Pink
Right hand "P," palm in, moves down on lips with middle finger, twice

Yellow
Start right hand "Y" palm out to side; pivot in toward body, twice

Red
Index finger of right hand "1" bends down across lips into "X" shape, twice

Blue
"B" hand open, palm out, pivoting back and forth at wrist

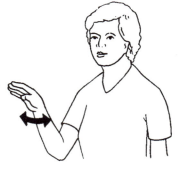

Purple
Pivot right hand "P" back and forth at wrist, twice

Gold

Start right hand "sensing" shape with palm to side of face; rotate wrist until palm faces out

Silver

Little finger of right, palm-down "S" hand draws line (from thumb-side out) along knuckles of left, palm-down "A" hand

Light

Start both hands pressed together at finger/thumb tips; pull open wide up and out — *also* "Bright"

Dark

Both "5" hands start fingers pointing up, palms facing body, then cross, moving downward — *also* "Dim"

Time, Tempo, and Pace

Fast

"1" hands start pointing out, palms facing, left hand further out than right; hands quickly move up and into "X" shape — *also* "Quick," "Rapid"

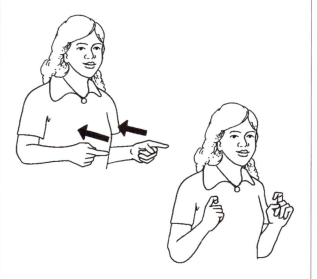

Slow

Fingers of open right hand draw slowly from back of left hand past wrist

Before

Both bent "B" hands; start back of right in palm of left, then move right hand closer to body

After

Both closed "5" hands; right hand, palm left, crosses in downward motion over back of left hand, palm down

Done

Both "5" hands start palms up; curve down and out broadly, ending with palms angled out and down — *also* "Finished"

Sometimes

With palm in, right index finger circles above left palm repeatedly — *also* "Occasionally" — *Note:* modify this sign by changing the speed of the movement and the number of repetitions to match your meaning

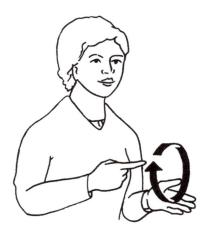

Often

Start palm of slightly bent "B" right hand facing left, right fingertips on open left palm; move left hand in bouncing motion foreword repeatedly

Daily

Hold "A" hand to cheek, thumb pointing back; move twice from cheek forward to just in front of face

Never

Right hand "B" starts palm left, arcs right and forward, then down straight

Short (in duration)

Both "H" hands, palms in; right fingers start at first knuckle of left index finger and slide along finger out and back several times

Later

Thumb of "L" hand starts palm down, moves down pivoting slightly until palm is left — *also* "After a while"

Late

Holding right arm out to side, bend "B" hand back and forth several times — *also* "Not yet," "Haven't"

Next

Start both hands open, palms in, right closer to body; move right up and over in front of left

Forever

Right hand "1" starts at midchest, moves in small circle toward right shoulder; changing to "Y," arcs down, away from body, and palm down

Final

Right hand "I" starts palm in at upper chest, moves down, turn palm up and striking little finger of palm-in left hand "I" — *also* "Last"

Yet

Both hands start fingers pointing up, pivot at wrists until palms down and out — *also* "Still"

Recent

Right hand "B" brushes against jawline repeatedly; the more recent the event, the more scrunched the shoulder

Now

With thumbs and small fingers extended, palms facing body, bring hands straight down into bent "B" handshapes

Future

Right hand "B" starts palm left, beside face at eye level, and moves out

Past

Right hand "B" pats toward back of right shoulder

Early

Move bent right middle finger up across back of palm down left hand

Always

Index finger of right "1" hand, pointing up, moves in counterclockwise circle

Local

Left hand "O," right hand "B"; right palm down, right circles once just above left

Far

Start both "A" hands, thumbs extended up, palms facing, knuckles touching; move right hand forward in arc

Near

Both bent, closed "5" hands; move right hand from near body out to left palm — *also* "Close"

Together

Both "A" hands start with knuckles together, thumbs up, move together in horizontal, clockwise circle

Absent

Claw "5" hand begins palm toward face; moves down through and past left hand claw "5," closing

Up

Point extended index finger up, palm left

Down

Point and move extended finger straight down — *also* "Downstairs"

Right (direction)

Move right hand "R" out to right, palm out

Left

Left hand "L" with palm out moves left

West

"W" hand at shoulder height moves right to left

East

"E" hand at shoulder height moves left to right

North

"N" hand, palm out, moves up to just a little above shoulder height

South

"S" hand, palm out, moves down at right of body from just a little above shoulder to just above waist

5. Other Parts of Signing

The Signs for:
- *Questions and Answers*
- *Pronouns, Indexers, and Other Stand-ins*
- *Conjunctions and Prepositions*
- *Etiquette*

Special Issues

Pronouns

There is a universal sign that covers most English pronouns: *I/me, you, he/him, she/her, it, we/us, they/them/those.* Simplistically stated, this sign consists of the signer pointing to the person, called *indexing.*

But what does a signer do when referring to a person who is not actually present? They establish a spatial marker to stand in for the person. For instance, let's say you are signing an anecdote about Elvira. The first time you refer to her, you might fingerspell her name, use her sign name if she has one, or do both, particularly if the person you're signing with doesn't know Elvira or if she has a common name sign. That first time you refer to Elvira, you point to a space, usually on your non-dominant side. That spot will henceforth stand in for Elvira. Each subsequent time you refer to Elvira (she/her), you point to where you placed Elvira earlier.

There is also a way in which a signer *stands in* for the person they are describing, particularly when they describe someone speaking or performing an action. To make it clear who they are describing, the signer shifts into a slightly different stance with each character. Let's say the signer is relating a three-way interchange held earlier among Joe and Mary and himself. When relating what he himself said, the signer would take a stance with his body held straight toward the receiver; the stance for Joe might be with the upper body angled slightly to the right; and for Mary, the signer's body is angled slightly to the left. The signer then will always shift his body into the appropriate stance as the narration proceeds from the signer to Joe to Mary and back.

This would be highly difficult if not impossible to demonstrate by line drawings! However, after a little signing time with experienced signers, you'll catch on. In the meantime, if your library has video tapes on signing, avail yourself of these. Books and videos can be invaluable resources.

Prepositions

In English, prepositions are words that show the position or relation of one thing to another — *of, by, in, on, under, to,* and so on. Prepositions do exist in ASL, and we include them here but with a disclaimer: prepositions are "English"; if you think of using them in Sign the same way you use prepositions in English, you are doomed to go astray. In Sign, multiple individual prepositions between signs simply are not a part of routine discourse. A good signer will incorporate the prepositional concept into his or her other signs. For instance, to sign "put the book on the table" the signs for *put, book,* and *table* will be modified and used directionally to show the motion of book to table; no separate preposition is needed.

Having made the above disclaimer, in truth, experienced signers *do* use prepositions sometimes. They use them if they are signing in English order. As a beginner, you may sometimes be forced to resort to them if you are unsure of how to incorporate the prepositional concept into some other sign. In any case, signers should be directional when signing positional concepts. That is, indicate position and relation not by inserting prepositional signs, but by directing your signs in a way that communicates the *sense* of what you're expressing.

Note also that the prepositional signs themselves, when you do use them, are highly directional in nature. For instance, the signs for *beneath* and *above* (p.199) are basically the same sign, with a changed location of the dominant hand. It's important that you alter your prepositional signs — by hand location, palm orientation, direction of movement (not handshape) — as you learned earlier to do with verbs to show the specific relationship between two particular things. For instance, to indicate that something is "on the wall," move your hands up where the wall is, don't just sign *on* the one way we have shown in our dictionary. Make sure your hands reflect your meaning accurately.

Questions

This last part of the dictionary contains the question words: *Who, Why, How,* and so on. When you sign a question, facial expression and body stance are very important. There are two basic question types in Sign that require two types of facial expression.

First, there are the "Yes/No" questions (to which a "yes" or "no" answer is required). When asking a "Yes/No" question, you should lean forward and raise your eyebrows.

Second, there are all other questions (*Who, What, When, Where, Why,* and also *How*), called the "WH" questions. When asking a "WH" question you should lower/furrow your eyebrows; in fact, do so to an extreme that most hearing people read as angry or perturbed. Also make sure to lean forward.

You may also use the drawn question mark (see the dictionary entry for *question*) at the end *or* at the beginning of any type of question. But whether or not you do, you **must** shape your eyebrows to create the appropriate facial expression for the specific kind of question you are asking. (Notice the faces of signers of the question words in this part of the dictionary.)

Other Parts of Signing

Questions and Answers

Question
Draw question mark: start with right index finger up, palm out and end palm down, finger pointing out

Who
Folded "3" hand opens and closes at mouth — *Note:* notice other two signs for "Who;" all three are commonly used

Who
Thumb and forefinger of "C" hand open and close at mouth

Who
"1" index finger draws circle around mouth

What
Both "5" hands palm up, with the appropriate questioning expression

What if? Suppose
"I" hand starts palm in at temple and moves out slightly

Where
Right hand "1," palm out, rocks back and forth

When

Both "1" hands, right palm down, left palm up; right index finger half circles above tip of left index finger, then tips touch — *Note:* do not use as "When we were young"

Why

With right hand palm in, wriggle middle finger of "5" hand toward self

How much?

Press backs of knuckles of both hands together ("how"); pull hands apart and up ("much")

What time (is it)?

Right hand "X" taps back of left wrist

How

Start hands palms in, back of knuckles pressed together; roll hands over and up until palms are up and backs of fingers together

No

Extended index and middle fingers come together with thumbs, twice

Not

"A" hand starts with thumb under chin and moves forward — *also* "Don't," "Doesn't"

Yes

"S" hand nods forward at wrist several times

Maybe

Both closed "5" hands, palm up; start with right hand low and left hand high; move right up and left down, then back to where they were

Pronouns, Indexers, and Other Stand-ins

He, Him, She, Her, It, They, Them

Pointing (indexing) toward the referred thing or being, or its spatial marker is ASL's version of *pronouns* in English

I, Me

Right index finger points to midchest (or more emphatically, may tap)

Myself

"A" hand taps midchest — *Note:* this is an indexing sign; change hand position to indicate "yourself," "himself," and so on

My

Closed "5" hand, thumb up, presses (or more emphatically, taps) midchest

You

"1" hand extends with palm down — *Note:* for plural, point at several spots

Yours, Hers, His, Theirs

Right hand "B" moves slightly out — *Note:* the use of this sign, similar to the indexing sign, should be made clear by context and spatial markers

Those

Right hand "1" points at right temple, then pivots at wrist and finger arcs slightly until palm is out

We

Right hand "1" starts bent at the wrist, palm in, finger pointing left; hand arcs left and forearm pivots until palm is out

Us

Right hand "U" starts palm left; hand and arm curve around in front of body until palm faces right

Our

Right hand bent "B" starts palm left; hand and arm curve around in front of body until palm faces right

Something

With thumb up, move right hand closed "5" first toward body, then move right in gentle arcs and end with palm up

Someone

Point extended finger up and circle forearm repeatedly, keeping palm facing body — *also* occasionally used as "Something"

Thing

Move upturned, slightly bent "B" hand in arc from center of body to right

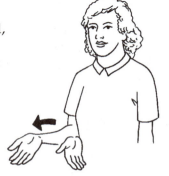

Nothing

Right hand "5" starts under chin, then moves down, opening, and out

Here

Both "5" hands, palms up, move in small circles at midchest

There

Point index finger at specific location

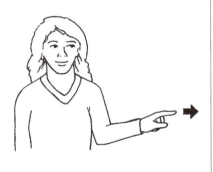

Conjunctions
and
Prepositions

From
Right "X" finger starts touching left, extended up index finger, then moves right

About
(on the topic)
Move right "H" hand around left "H" hand

Out
Start left hand "C" clasping wrist of right hand "5"; right hand rises up through left, closing into flattened "O" shape — *also* "Outside," but do twice

Out
Start right hand "5," palm up, in palm of left hand "C"; right hand moves out and away from body and into "flattened O" shape — *Note:* this sign should always be modified to accurate-

In, Into
Right fingers go into and through cup of left hand "C" — *also* "Enter"

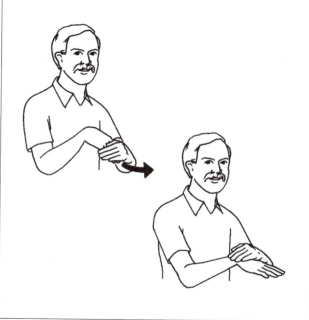

Behind

Start both "A" hands, palms facing; move right hand from in front of left hand to behind left hand

Between

Insert right hand "B" between middle and ring fingers of left hand "B" and rock right hand back and forth slightly

Beneath

Start right hand "A" above palm-down left closed "5" hand; move right hand underneath left — *also* "Under," "Below"

Above

Circle right hand "B" above left hand "B"

Against

Right hand bent "B" strikes palm of left hand "B" — *also* "Opposed"

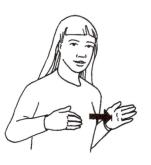

With

Both "A" hands start apart, palms facing, then move together

Toward

Start both "1" hands apart at midchest, palms facing; right hand arcs over to almost touch left index finger

Around

Extended right index finger, pointing down, circles flattened "O" left hand — *Note:* do not use to mean "Approximately"

During

Both "1" index fingers extended, point forward, then move down and out in slight arc

Because

Start right index finger at right forehead; bring out in slight arc, closing into "A" shape — *Note:* see variation; both are commonly used

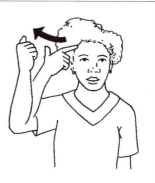

Because

Start right hand closed "5" at right forehead; bring out in slight arc, closing into "A" shape

Except

With right hand "F," tug up on left index finger — *also* "Special"

Or

Right hand "1," left "L," palms toward body; right index finger touches left thumb then left index finger — *Note:* use when describing a specific choice, such as "This one" or "That one"

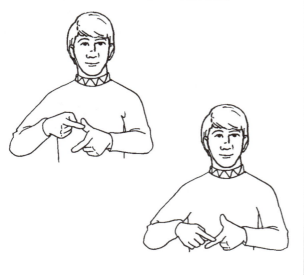

For

Index finger starts palm in at temple; wrist pivots until palm is out and finger up at angle

And

Start "claw" hand below left shoulder; pull right and close into flattened "O"

Etiquette

Hello
Start bent fingers of right hand at forehead, move out

(Are you) Coming?
Both "1" hands, index fingers angled down, palms in, start just above waist and arc left and down toward body

Good-bye
Fingers of right hand start open, pointing up, then bend up and down repeatedly

Take care
Both "K" hands, palms facing; right hand taps down on top of left

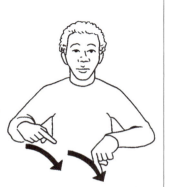

Thank you
Right hand "B" begins in front of mouth, moves down and out, turning palm up — *Note:* use two hands for a more emphatic "Thanks"

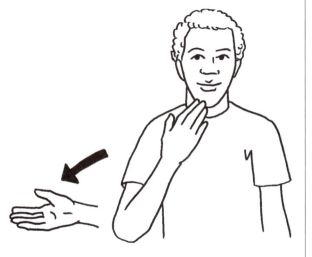

Please
Right hand "B," palm in, makes small circle at mid-chest

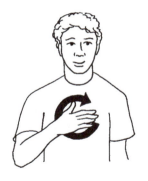

Excuse (me)

Right fingertips brush along open left palm and straight out ends of left fingertips — *also* "Pardon," "Forgive"

Sorry

"A" hand, palm in, moves in a circle at midchest, repeatedly

Welcome

Start open right hand up, palm in, at side; sweep down and left, ending palm up

V. Putting It All Together

Like any language, ASL has a set of rules and conventions about how signs are assembled to convey meaning. We could devote many chapters to the complexities and subtleties of tense, syntax, and other aspects of the grammar of ASL, but it's debatable whether such information would be useful to a beginning signer. Certainly it would be beyond the goal of this book, which is to provide some simple guidelines to getting started in ASL. If you wish to become involved in more depth in a linguistically detailed study of ASL, many books have been written on the subject. *Sign Language Made Simple*, however, is a basic dictionary of ASL, and is not meant to be an in-depth explanation of the grammar, syntax, and structure of this complex language.

But you do need something with which to get started, especially in the area of word order. The order of signs in ASL bears very little relation to the word order in English sentences. For example, as mentioned in Section 4 of the dictionary, signs used as modifiers (adjectives) normally follow the signs they modify, an order that resembles Romance languages more than it does English. Basically, what this means is that you would say *brown dog* but you would sign *dog brown*. In addition, modifiers, especially those that modify verbs, are very often indicated by a modification to the verb sign itself. So where you might say *slow dance*, in ASL you would execute the movement for the sign *dance*, but do so much more languorously than you would to describe a jig.

A signed communication will always be presented in a strikingly different manner than the same basic content would be in English. If you take a sentence in English and try to express it literally in ASL — that is, present a sign for each word, down to each *a, and,* and *into,* in the same order as English — you will not make sense; you will make perhaps an understandable pidgin mess. The same is true when you are being signed to; take off your "English lenses" and try to absorb the wholeness of what is being signed rather than translating it into words.

We're going to demonstrate word order through example rather than by listing rules. Look carefully at the next signs/sentences; they are excellent examples of the natural order of signs in ASL.

The classic typing-class drill is chock-full of modifiers: "The quick brown fox jumped over the lazy dog." Here's how to sign it in ASL:

Dog

Lazy

Lying Down
(the dog)

Fox

Brown

Quick

Jumping Over

Here's another example. Let's say you watched a signer present the following signs, and you understood the basic meaning of each sign.

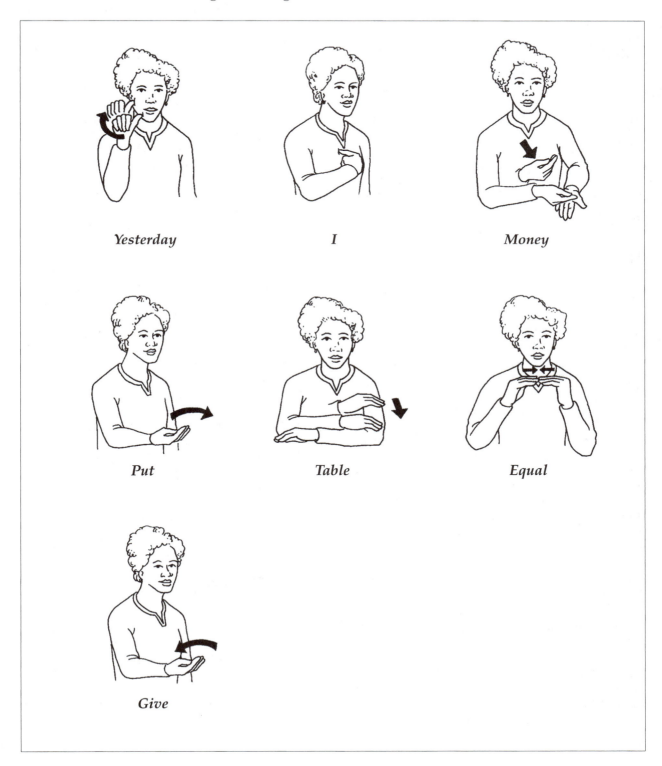

Yesterday   *I*   *Money*

Put   *Table*   *Equal*

Give

If you were to jot down the word equivalent of each sign (a very "English"/linear way of thinking to start with) what you'd end up with as an English sentence would be nonsensical. You would *not* get the sentence "Give me the same amount of money I put on the table yesterday," which is the more sensible English version. That's because no two languages on earth can be mechanically translated word-for-word with good result. You can't do it from French to German, and you can't do it from ASL to English.

With signing, you may at first find yourself feeling (accustomed as you are to thinking in English) that something is missing. Ignore that feeling, and try not to give in to the urge to supply the missing pieces! It is all there already. Look at this sentence again:

Give me the same amount of money I put on the table yesterday.

We've underlined what you might view as missing in the signed version — no precise signs for these were in the signing. Yet these concepts *are* communicated in the signs. Look again.

Is *me* missing? No, the way the signer signs *give* shows direction; who is giving to whom is clear. What about *the*? Not necessary; articles (such as *a, and,* and *the*) are entirely irrelevant in ASL. They serve to link, connect, and relate words to words in English; hand movement does that in signing. The same is true about *of*. Similarly it is not necessary to sign *on the* before *table*. The way the signer directs his or her hands shows the direction toward the table.

Remember: Don't use this or any other signing dictionary as a "translator." You cannot simply substitute signs for each word in English sentences.

In truth, ASL has more in common with other spoken languages (such as Spanish) than it does to English. English is notoriously difficult to grasp as a second language, particularly when it comes to prepositions (*on, in, by, of,* and so on). Linguistically, English is probably a lot more complicated than it needs to be; certainly, it seems to have more rules (and those rules have more exceptions) than many other Western languages do.

As we've talked about before, a striking difference between ASL and English is in the use of modifiers. We have talked repeatedly about the reason for this: many signs are signed directionally or are modified. These modifications incorporate the prepositions and modifiers into the central noun or verb sign. You simply don't alter English words that way, so in English you must string together more words to get the meaning across! The end result in signing is that you get all the shifts and refinements of meaning as in English, but many of the separate "little words" become superfluous. They do exist, but in pure ASL you won't see them.

To summarize, in English, precision of meaning is communicated almost exclusively through the combined meanings of individual words; for more meaning, you add more words. In ASL, the individual signs convey a general meaning; when you want enhanced meaning, you sometimes add new signs, but often (especially with modifiers) you alter the signs to incorporate the additional meaning. Furthermore, without adding more signs, you incorporate refinements of meaning through body stance and facial expression. Always keep this in mind and remember that you simply cannot pick and choose signs from this or any other signing dictionary and string them together "English fashion."

The Grammar of Facial Expression

As you experiment with communicating in ASL, it is vital that you keep your face involved. Remember, facial expression serves as a grammatical aspect of signing. While many of the faces in our dictionary of signs bear a somewhat neutral expression, ASL does not allow for a blank or neutral expression. The dictionary faces are on a page; they have no context. They are signing generic, dictionary-correct signs. A person signing something specific will always have a context. You *must* use your face to impart meaning in tandem with the meaning being imparted by your hands. If you are asking a question, show it with the appropriate facial expression. (The expressions appropriate for certain kinds of questions are explained in the Special Issues text that begins Section 5 of the Dictionary.) Often the intensity on the faces of signers seems exaggerated to outsiders, but this extreme expressiveness is proper and is a vital ingredient of the language. (Deaf people often find the faces of hearing people strangely inexpressive!) If you are expressing revulsion, grimace and turn your mouth down. Don't think of your descriptive facial expressions as bells and whistles; they are part of the underlying structure of ASL.

Negatives

When expressing something negative when signing, adding the sign for *not* works fine in many cases. Keep this in mind before you look in the index for words that start with the prefixes *dis* or *un* or *anti*. If the root word is in the dictionary, you can use it plus *not* to form its negative (antonym). For instance:

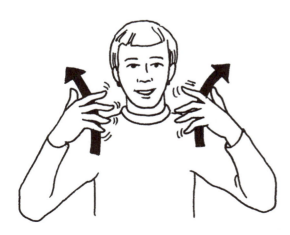

Friendly

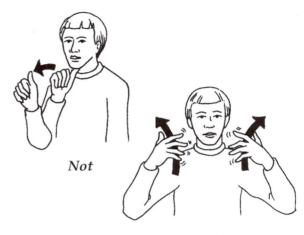

Not

Friendly

Sometimes you will have a choice. There is a separate antonym sign *false* to signify the opposite of *true*; or, you may use *not* with *true*.

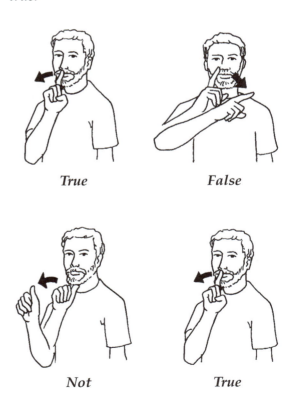

True   *False*

Not   *True*

Another way to show negation is to sign, but as you are doing so shake your head *no*.

Notice the faces. When forming negatives, it is vital to use not just manual information, but non-manual markers as well. Always accompany negative information by shaking your head from side to side or by reinforcing it in other ways: scrunch up your facial features; frown; or, if you are expressing something negative but sympathy or anger is part of the equation; express those things with your face. *No* with regret is different from *No* with anger.

This point cannot be emphasized too strongly: using facial expressions clearly and appropriately is a *required* part of the grammar of signing, not an option.

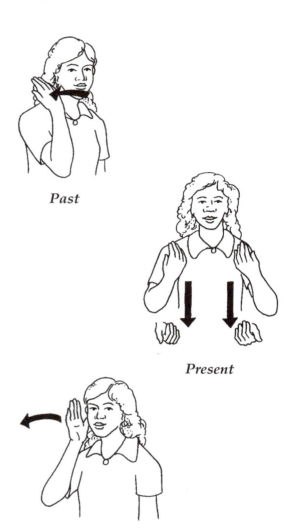

Past

Present

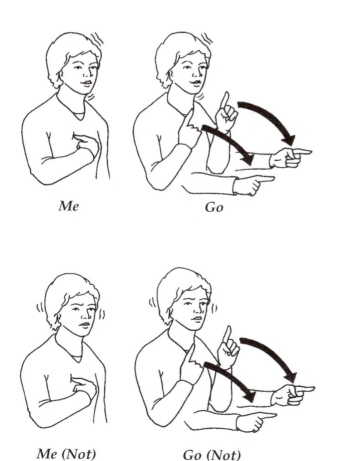

Me

Go

Future

Me (Not)

Go (Not)

Tense

Showing tense is in some ways easier in signing than in English, with all its irregular verbs. When you begin signing the most basic ASL, for instance, it is perfectly acceptable for you to show tense like this: at the beginning of your discourse, simply indicate the time context by indicating *past, present*, or *future* with the appropriate sign.

Here's an example. You want to sign the equivalent of this English sentence: "I studied so I am not nervous about the test. I'll be celebrating tonight." Here's what you'll do:

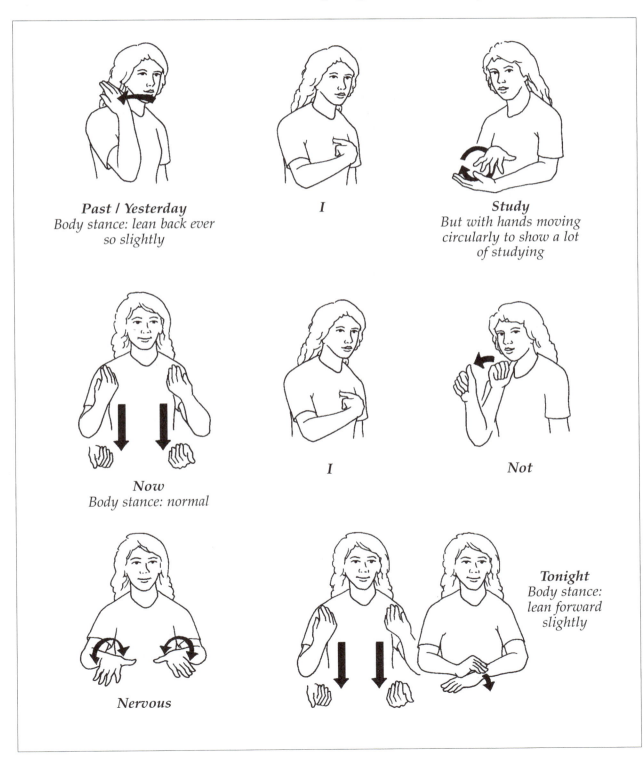

Past / Yesterday
Body stance: lean back ever so slightly

I

Study
But with hands moving circularly to show a lot of studying

Now
Body stance: normal

I

Not

Nervous

Tonight
Body stance: lean forward slightly

I

Celebrate
*With hands moving
circularly to show
much partying*

When signing, keep in mind as you go that the receivers are noting mentally when a tense is established. Make sure when you change tense in mid-discourse that you make it clear by signing, for instance, *yesterday* or *past* or *tomorrow*, and also by shifting stance. By comparison, an English listener is reminded of tense at every occurrence of a verb; signers must be conscious of establishing (reestablishing) tense, too.

Putting It All Together

Now here's what you've been waiting for: examples of putting it all together in some simple, classic verses, sayings, and more. First, here are the first few signs you might exchange with a deaf person to whom you've just been introduced.

Hi!

Are you hearing?
(versus deaf)

Nice

Meet

You

In the other examples that follow, notice the great differences between the signed verse and the English verse. The differences are great, but nevertheless, signers certainly get the message across, and with the particular spice of ASL. As you enjoy these examples and experiment with signing, remember that these signers are exercising poetic license as they sign. That is not to say that the signs are in any way inaccurate. But if you compare some of the signs here to their counterparts that appear in the dictionary, you'll notice that they are not identical. (For instance, compare the dictionary entry for *list* and the signing of *list the ways* in the first quotation by Elizabeth Barrett Browning.) That is partly because of poetic license; it's also partly because signs have been appropriately directed and modified for the context of the material — an essential part of the grammar of ASL.

How do I love thee? Let me count the ways.
I love thee to the depth and breadth and height
My soul can reach...

E. Barrett Browning
Sonnets from the Portuguese

How much	*I*	*Love*
You	*List the ways*	*I*

"How do I love thee..."
      Continued

Love

You

Same

My

Soul

Deep

Broad

High

Train up a child in the way he should go and when he is old he will not depart from it.
Proverbs 22:6

Raise up

Child

How

Should

Become (1)

Become (2)

Become (3)

And

When / Happen

"Train up a child in the way he should go..."
Continued

Old

He

Won't

Depart

From

How

Raise

To every thing there is a season, and a time to every purpose under heaven.

Ecclesiastes 3:1

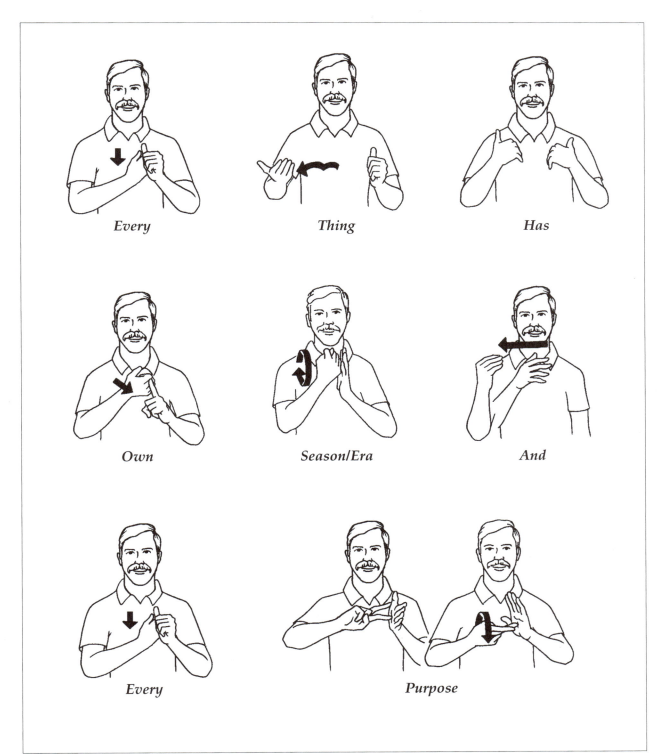

Every	Thing	Has
Own	Season/Era	And
Every	Purpose	

"To every thing there is a season..."
                                    Continued

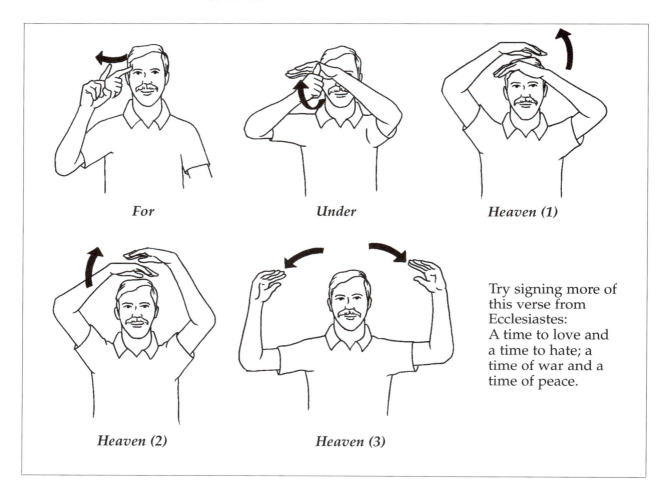

For   *Under*   *Heaven (1)*

Heaven (2)   *Heaven (3)*

Try signing more of
this verse from
Ecclesiastes:
A time to love and
a time to hate; a
time of war and a
time of peace.

The cautious seldom err.
                    Confucius, *The Analects*, 4:23

People   *Careful*

"The cautious seldom err..."
Continued

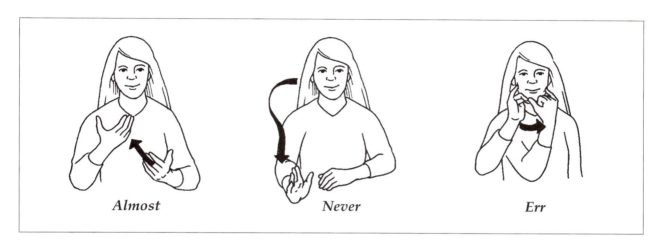

A penny saved is a penny earned.
Ben Franklin, *Poor Richard's Almanac*

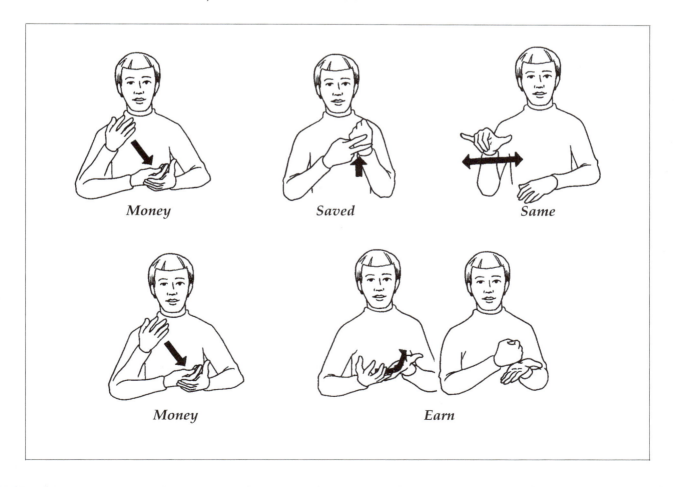

Appearances are often deceiving.
>   Aesop, *The Wolf in Sheep's Clothing*

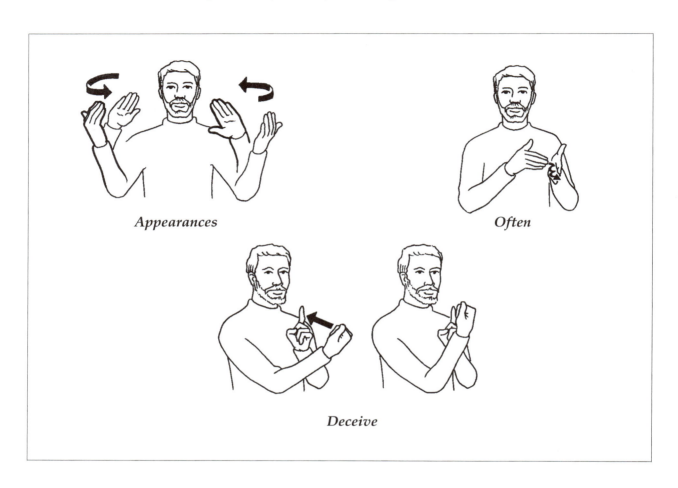

Appearances

Often

Deceive

Time is money.
>   Ben Franklin, *Poor Richard's Almanac*

Time   **Equal**   **Money**

Try signing:
Eat to live,
not live to eat
(also from
*Poor Richard's
Almanac*).

Familiarity breeds contempt.
    Aesop, *The Fox and the Lion*

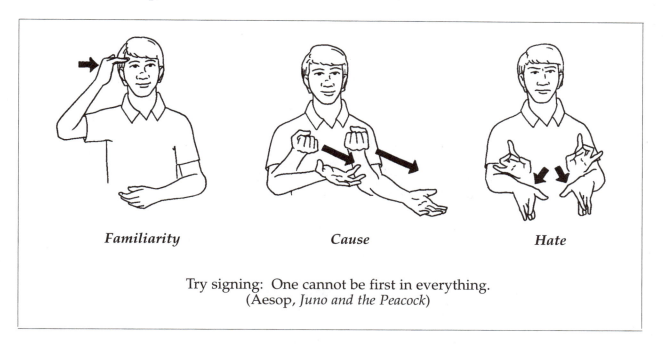

Familiarity   **Cause**   **Hate**

Try signing: One cannot be first in everything.
(Aesop, *Juno and the Peacock*)

Slow and steady wins the race.
    Aesop, *The Hare and the Tortoise*

Slow   **Win**

Continuous/Steady   **Race**

Absence makes the heart grow fonder.
first attributed to Sextus Aurelius Propertius, b. 54 BC

Absence   *Cause*   *Heart*

Become

More   *Cherished*   *Attached*

Have no friends not equal to yourself.
  Confucius, *The Analects*, 1:8, iii

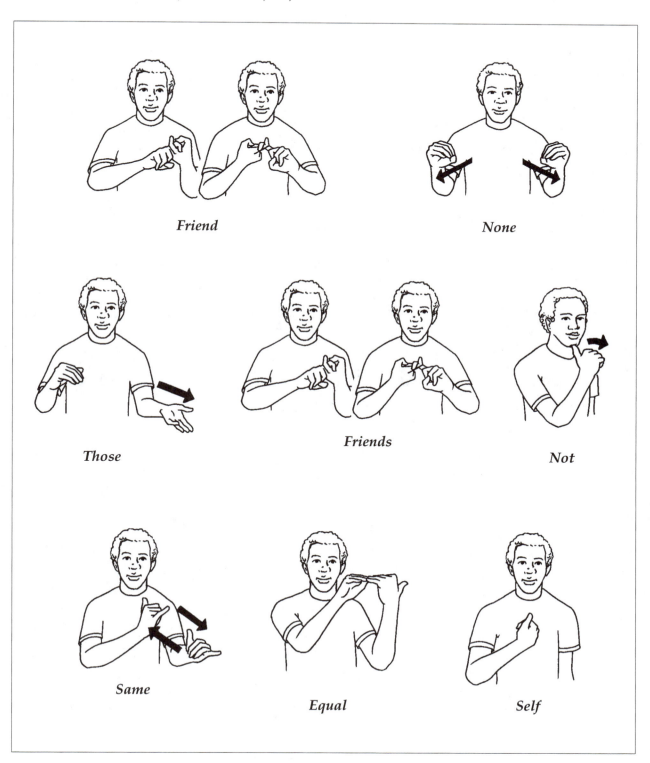

Friend

None

Those

Friends

Not

Same

Equal

Self

The Lord's Prayer
    from the New Testament, the King James Version (Matthew 6:9-13)

Our Father which art in heaven,
Hallowed be thy name,
Thy kingdom come,
Thy will be done,
In earth as it is in Heaven.
Give us this day our daily bread.
And forgive us our debts,
As we forgive our debtors.
And lead us not into temptation,
But deliver us from evil.
For thine is the kingdom, and the
Power, and the glory, for ever,
Amen.

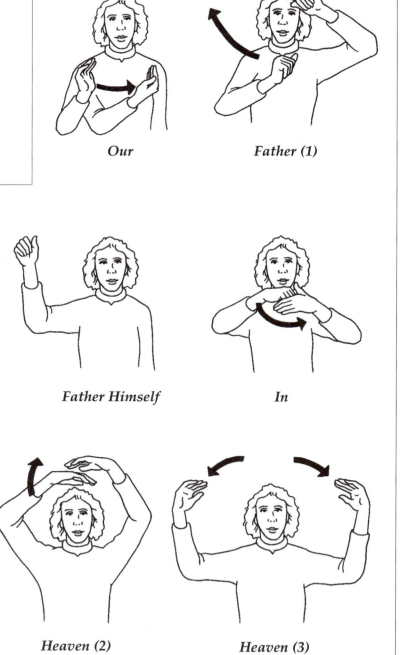

Our   *Father (1)*

Father (2)   *Father Himself*   *In*

Heaven (1)   *Heaven (2)*   *Heaven (3)*

The Lord's Prayer
Continued

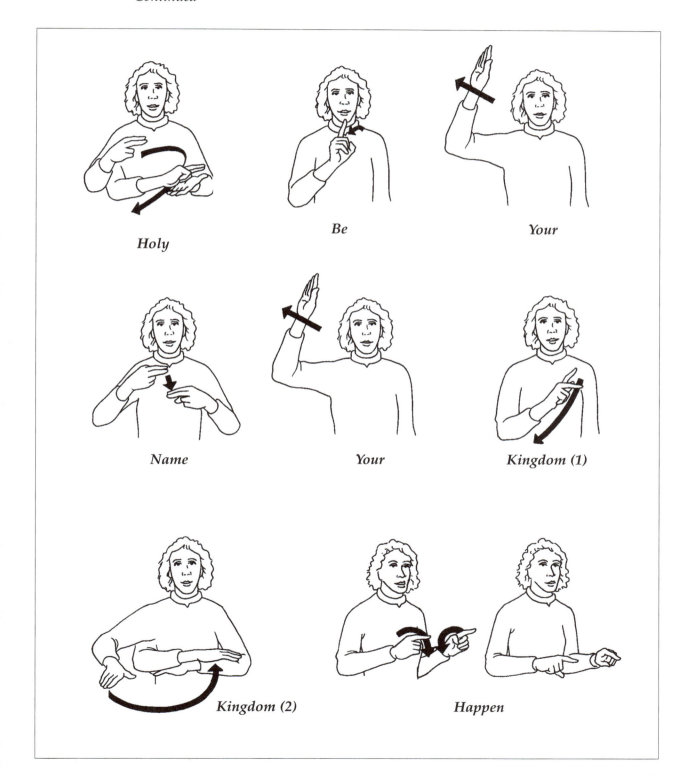

Holy

Be

Your

Name

Your

Kingdom (1)

Kingdom (2)

Happen

The Lord's Prayer
        Continued

Your

Want / Will

Finish / Done

Here (Earth)

Same

Heaven (1)

Heaven (2)

The Lord's Prayer
Continued

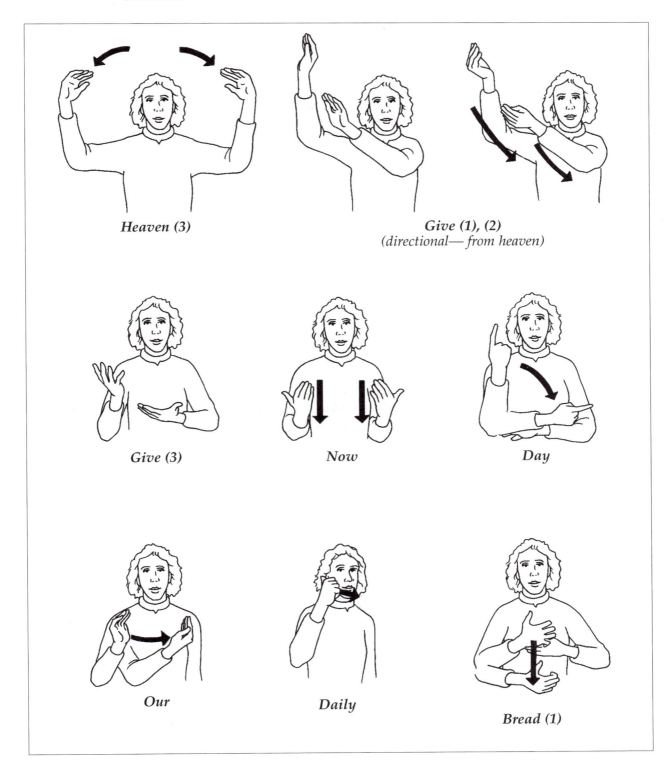

Heaven (3)

Give (1), (2)
(directional— from heaven)

Give (3)

Now

Day

Our

Daily

Bread (1)

The Lord's Prayer
Continued

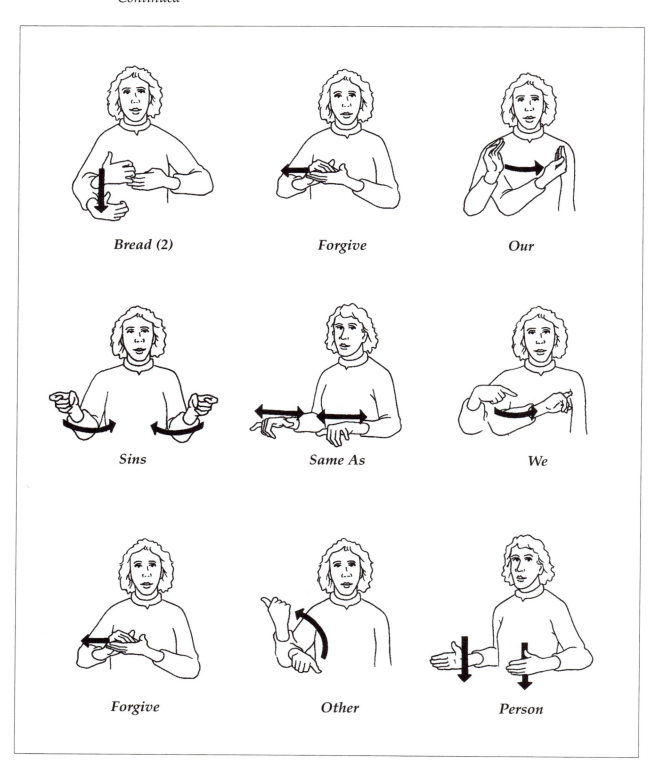

Bread (2)

Forgive

Our

Sins

Same As

We

Forgive

Other

Person

The Lord's Prayer
Continued

Sins

Prevent

Us

Fall into

Temptation

Save / Deliver

Us

From

Evil

The Lord's Prayer
    Continued

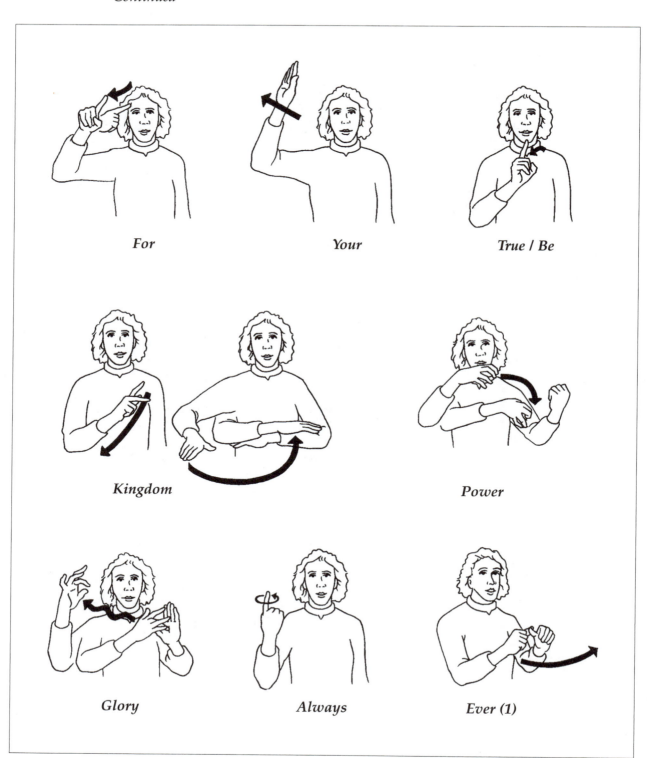

For

Your

True / Be

Kingdom

Power

Glory

Always

Ever (1)

The Lord's Prayer
Continued

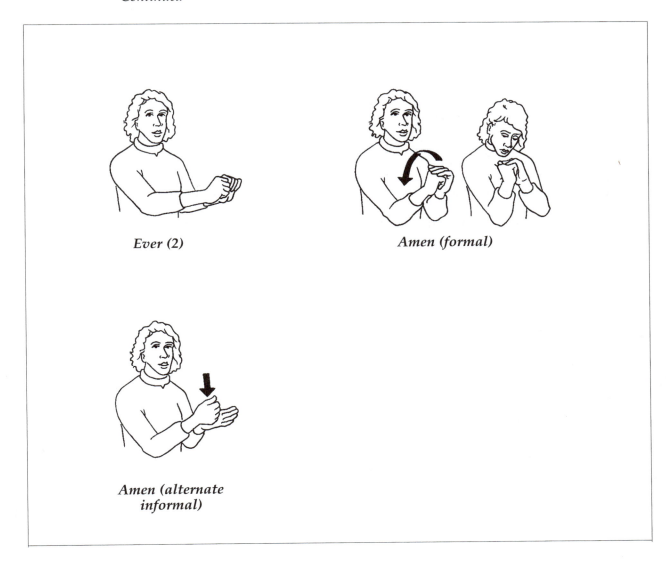

Ever (2)

Amen (formal)

*Amen (alternate
informal)*

VI. Humor, Piquancy, and Vulgarity

Just as there are "plays on words," signers use and combine signs in creative and humorous ways to create puns, witticisms, double entendres, and outright vulgarities.

For instance, as you've noticed, we've occasionally presented two or more equally acceptable ways to sign a particular concept. Sometimes these are regional differences, sometimes a second sign will emerge purely as a pun sign. For instance, compare the following two signs for *understand*.

The first of these signs is the regular sign for the concept. The second is purely playful. This more playful sign alludes to the concept by playing on the sign for *stand*. It is, in fact, the sign for *stand* turned upside down so that the legs of the right hand are standing under rather than on top of the left hand (as they do for the sign *stand*).

In terms of sheer wit, however, there are few "sign plays" that rival the one for *weekend*. While there is a dictionary sign for *weekend*, the one below shows an entirely different version. Notice how the right hand is walking over one of the "ends" of the body. Hmmm...wonder if that hand is walking over the strong end or over the weak end?

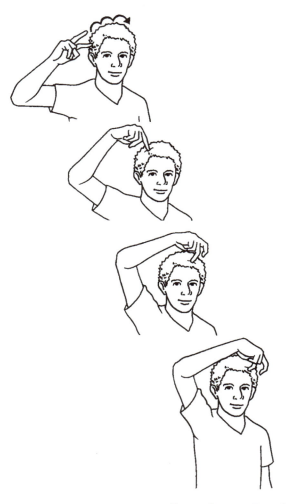

Over the weekend

Understand

Understand

The next few pages are filled with signs and sign stories that demonstrate amply that English speakers have no patent on showing off their sense of humor through language.

WOW!

This is a great, fun sign. Not only do the two "W" hands and the "O" of the mouth spell WOW in English, it absolutely has a WOW! look about it.

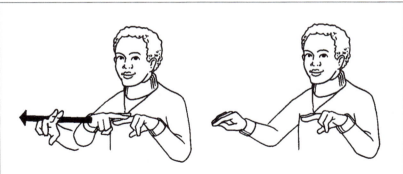

Never mind

Here's the sign for "train," but instead of making the standard back-and-forth motion, the right hand contiues off the left hand and out. What this sign literally means is "The train's gone." But it is used figuratively to say, "You've missed...Forget about it...Never mind."

Hopping from joint to joint

This sweet little pantomime is easy to get. That right hand is literally hopping from one (knuckle) joint to the other.

Bar hopping

Here the left fingers are the bars and the right fingers are doing the hopping.

Sears

Whether or not you shop at that venerable mercantile establishment, you must appreciate how the "S" hands and the signer's ears spell it out.

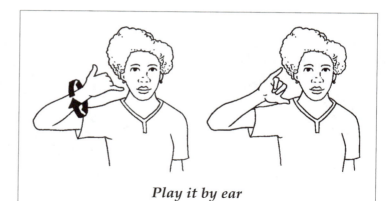

Play it by ear

Speaking of playful, this one takes the sign for "play," moves it up near the ear, and there you have it.

Pasteurized milk

This is one of the most witty and may be one of the most well-known plays on a sign. Start your right hand in an open "C" handshape to the right of your face, then move it slowly in front of your face (past your eyes — get it?), opening and closing it rhythmically from a "C" to an "S" shape, as if milking an udder.

Rule of thumb

Here, the basic sign for "rule" is used. But to signify not just "rule," but "rule of thumb," tap the right "R" hand not against the palm of the left hand, but the thumb only.

Golf

Finally, here's a word picture that describes golf in a way that's a lot like the alphabet stories. Certainly if would be a lot easier to simply fingerspell G O L F. But doesn't this series of signs convey the spirit of golf much better? (This is a lot like the alphabet/number series we show below.)

The left hand "G" serves as the tee for the right hand "O" (the ball).
Next the "L" handshape "swings" and "strikes."
Finally, the "F" hand shows the bouncing motion of the ball.

Humor and Names

To express names, ASL signers may fingerspell a name at first use during discourse or when they first meet someone. But this can be cumbersome in the flow of signing, especially when names are lengthy. Usually, friends and family and any folks who sign together on a frequent basis will give each other shortcut sign names for efficiency's sake, and these names have a way of sticking around for life.

Do note one important cultural aspect of sign names: You can't give yourself one! That would be as wrong headed as nicknaming yourself. The only real way to acquire a sign name is to have one bestowed on you by your deaf friends. In addition to being efficient, if you are given a sign name by your deaf friends it will either say something specific about you or a lot about how you are viewed by signers. For instance, look at the sign names for Presidents Reagan and Carter, Shakespeare, and Laurent Clerc (the first deaf person to teach deaf students in the United States).

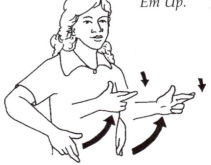

Two sign names for Ronald Reagan. First, the "R" hand cuts the throat; or, there's Ronald Reagan as "Mr. Shoot 'Em Up."

Two sign names for Jimmy Carter

First, there he is grinning his toothy grin. In an alternate sign name, the signer uses a "C" hand to make the sign for "nuts." (The standard "nuts" is shown by the female signer.)

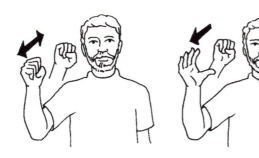

Shakespeare?? Yep. This sign demonstrates how to hold, shake, and throw a spear.

On a more serious note, this is the name sign for Laurent Clerc, the Frenchman who was the first deaf person to teach deaf students in the United States. The "H" hand strokes the cheek, indicating the scar that was on Clerc's face.

ABC and Number Stories

Signers have fun playing around with their language in ways that are similar to palindromes or rhyming riddles in English. For amusement, signers have created and continue to come up with little stories or sayings in which the handshapes start with "1", then "2", then "3", and so on. Similarly, the handshapes might proceed alphabetically, going from "A" to "B" and so on. Some have even been created that include the entire alphabet! For purposes of demonstration, we're going to give a somewhat shorter example below. The captions beneath the signs are paraphrases only.

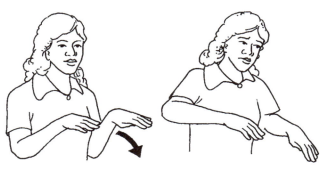

I revved my motorcycle
("A" hands)

But it screeched to a halt.
("B" hands)

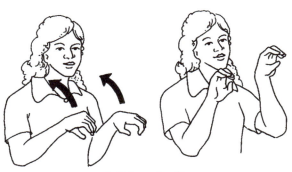

I did a wheelie.
("C" hands)

The speedometer went wild
("D" hands)

And the tires squealed!
("E" hands)

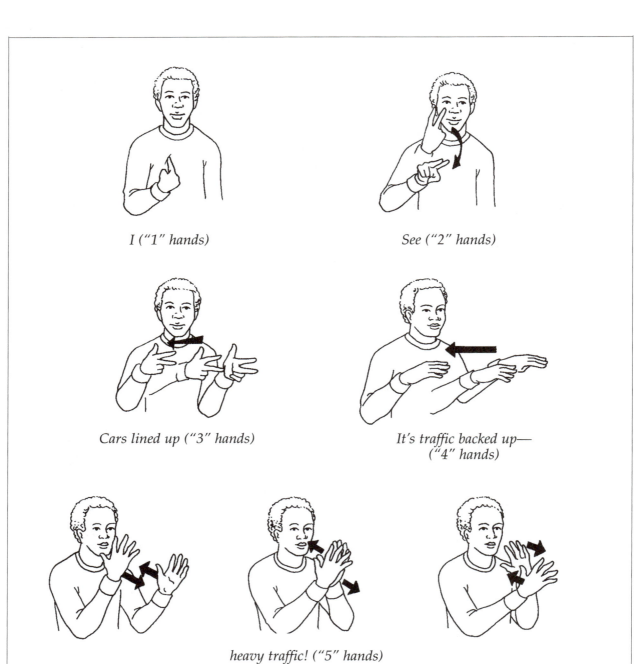

I ("1" hands)

See ("2" hands)

Cars lined up ("3" hands)

It's traffic backed up—
("4" hands)

heavy traffic! ("5" hands)

Vulgarities

Shame on you if you turned to this page first. One of the authors of this book, Karen Lewis, has run into too many ASL students who, before even learning to sign *Hello*, wanted to learn how to make signs for how to — nevermind, you get the drift. But there is just no wisdom in a beginning signer sashaying off with a loaded gun when they don't understand how many calibers it's got! Rest assured, there are signs so pornographic that they'll sizzle your fingernails, but we leave it to you to discover them.

Okay, okay. If you must sign naughty, here's a tidbit:

Bullshit

!@#$%!* (or darn, dangit, good grief, shit!)

Not that anyone *should* curse or use vulgarities, but as a beginner, you are all too likely to use them wrong. It is too easy to appear very foolish, and to be much more (or much less) offensive than you intend. The reason is that cursing, like idiomatic and metaphorical language, is highly culture-specific. It is very difficult to impart flare and sensitivity about these complex elements of language to a beginner in any language. If you are going take the low road (cursing) or the high road (poeticisms), you must pass your first miles on the middle road. And you must not just dabble in signing, but get acquainted with (if not submerged in) the deaf culture.

Finally, we offer these parting reminders about signing:

> Shape it right,
> Move it properly,
> Use your face,
> Sign what you mean,
> Have fun!

VII. Index

Italic page references indicate illustrations.

A

C